TENNIS SKILLS

TENNIS SKILLS

THE PLAYER'S GUIDE

TOM SADZECK

FIREFLY BOOKS

A FIREFLY BOOK

Library of Congress Cataloging in Publication Data is available

Canadian Cataloguing in Publication Data

Sadzeck, Tom
Tennis skills: the player's guide

ISBN 1-55209-494-4

1. Tennis – Literature. I. Title

Published in Canada in 2001
by Firefly Books Ltd.
3680 Victoria Park Avenue
Willowdale, Ontario, Canada
M2H 3K1

Published in the United States in 2001
by Firefly Books (U.S.) Inc.
P.O. Box 1338, Ellicott Station
Buffalo, New York, USA
14205

This book was designed and produced by
Quintet Publishing Limited
6 Blundell Street
London N7 9BH

Senior Project Editor: Laura Price
Editor: Andrew Armitage
Designers: Rod Teasdale, Sharanjit Dhol
Photography: Jamie Squire
Additional Photography: Allsport

Creative Director: Richard Dewing

Manufactured in Singapore by Regent Publishing Services
Printed in China by Lee-Fung Asco, Printers Ltd

Introduction

Most tennis enthusiasts will probably agree that few things come close to the pure satisfaction of hitting a tennis ball with power and control. Most of you reading this book have probably felt this satisfaction at some point in your tennis-playing experience and are now seeking advice on how to harness this magical feeling. Unfortunately you can't wave a magic wand or sprinkle any magic dust. It takes time, patience, and persistence to advance your game to the next level.

Most students have better success at developing their game when they begin to understand tennis concepts. A bigger picture needs to be painted in the mind's eye before a good understanding can occur. This big picture is created by the ability to see what it is you need to do with your game, how to do it, and how you can analyze it. You must take on the responsibility of becoming your own coach. Even if you take private lessons from a professional instructor you will still need to take the information he or she has given you and be able to translate it in your own way and on your own timetable.

You need to establish your own personal tennis program. This should include a good balance of conditioning, match play, rest, and practice. But not just practice: it has to be proper practice, which involves:

- development of fundamental stroke technique
- strategy
- isolation of common situations and patterns
- footwork drills
- understanding opponents' strengths and weaknesses
- mental training under pressure conditions
- maintaining stimulation through hours of repetition during these practice activities.

This may sound like a big mountain to climb, but with proper guidance and an optimistic outlook, you should be able to achieve a higher level of play.

This book is set up with this balance in mind. The first chapter provides basic instructional information on how to correctly hit a variety of shots. Whether you're just beginning to play the game or are an advanced player, you'll find the explanations simple and to the point. The photographs of professional players make it look easy as they demonstrate proper stroke technique.

The remainder of the book corresponds with the first chapter by allowing you to practice your stroke technique under various conditions. These conditions allow you to practice important aspects of your game such as consistency, accuracy, movement, timing, patterns, strategy, and pressure.

Throughout the book we'll talk a lot about the comparisons between the way the game is played at the professional level and the way it is played at the recreational level. A clear distinction should be understood from the outset. There are two important issues to point out. First of all, we need to watch what professionals are doing so that we can try to advance our level of play by copying their actions. I believe that the best way to learn is to watch or visualize a correct motion, and then try to imitate by repetition.

The second important issue is that professionals have been training for years against other top professionals. Recreational players have more limitations to their time and athletic ability. We need to keep this in perspective whenever we try to imitate Pete Sampras and his 120-m.p.h. (193 k.p.h.) serve. Recreational-level tennis is not quite the same, as we'll see throughout the book.

Tennis Talk

Before we get into the drills and skills, we need to acquaint ourselves with a few of the terms you'll hear time and time again on the courts. So here's a glossary.

Ace When a successful serve is untouched by the receiver.

Ad side The side of the court where the serve is made when the score is ad-in or ad-out.

Ad-in When the score indicates that the serving player or team has the "advantage."

Ad-out When the score indicates that the receiving player or team has the "advantage."

Advantage When the score indicates that the player or team that has the "advantage" has a chance to win the game by winning the next point.

Alley The area of the court between the singles and doubles sidelines.

Approach shot A shot attempt made near mid-court after the ball bounces short, and a player decides to continue to move forward toward the net.

Approach volley A shot attempt made near mid-court before the ball bounces, and a player decides to continue to move forward toward the net.

Backspin When a ball travels forward through the air while spinning underneath itself. Also called "slice."

Backswing The part of the groundstroke swing when the racket is taken back in preparation for moving forward through the swing.

Baseline The line at each end of the court extending from sideline to sideline.

Block volley A type of volley where a player reacts quickly by blocking the ball if it comes directly at the body.

Break point The situation when the player or team receiving serve has a chance to win the game on the point.

Center mark The short line extending from the center of each baseline toward the net.

Closed face When the racket face is angled down slightly toward the ground.

Closed stance The position of the body, when hitting a shot, where the feet and hips are turned more toward the side of the court.

Contact point The exact time when the racket meets the ball on any shot.

Continental grip The way the racket is held for specific shots such as a serve. Also called the "hammer" grip.

Deuce Refers to the score when it is tied at 40–40. Player or team must now win by two.

Deuce side The side of the court where the serve is made when the score is deuce.

Doubles sideline The lines on the side of the court at the outside of each alley.

Drop shot The shot after the ball bounces, when a player tries to hit the ball just barely over the net.

Drop volley The shot before the ball bounces, when a player tries to hit the ball just barely over the net.

Eastern backhand grip The way the racket is held for various types of backhand shots.

Eastern forehand grip The way the racket is held for various types of forehand shots. Sometimes referred to as a "shake-hands" grip.

Extreme backhand grip The way the racket is held specifically for a topspin backhand.

Flat This has two meanings: (1) when a ball travels forward through the air with very little or no spin; (2) the angle of the face of the racket when the strings are straight up and down.

Follow-through The part of the shot where the racket has completely finished hitting the ball.

Game Where the points are counted 15, 30, 40, then game. Games make sets, sets make a match.

Grip This has two meanings: (1) the part of the racket that you physically hold onto; (2) the position of the hand while holding the racket.

Groundstroke The shot when a player hits the ball after the bounce (usually occurs near the baseline).

Half-volley The shot when the ball is hit immediately after the bounce.

Hammer grip The way the racket should be held to take specific shots, such as a volley. This is also called the "continental" grip.

High-percentage shot Any shot attempt that is made when the odds are the greatest that the ball will land safely in the court.

Lob The shot when the ball is hit high into the air.

Loop Backswing A specific type of backswing where the racket head is initially brought back high, and then circles down below the ball before contact is made.

Love A term used in scoring which means "zero."

Low-percentage shot Any shot attempt that is made when the odds are the greatest that the ball will not land in the court.

Match The part of scoring when you have finished playing. Usually consists of winning two out of three sets. However, Grand Slam tournaments such as Wimbledon or the French Open play the best of five sets.

No-ad scoring A scoring system used where the score reaches "deuce," or 3–3, and the next point wins.

On the rise A specific way of hitting the ball as it is coming up from the bounce.

On-serve The situation where the score indicates that the serving player has won every game.

Open face When the racket face is angled up slightly toward the sky.

Open stance The position of the body, when hitting a shot, such that the feet and hips are turned toward the net.

Overhead smash The shot during the point when the ball is hit from above the head with a full swinging motion and follow-through. This usually occurs after a lob from the opponent.

Overswing When a player is hitting the ball excessively to the point where they are becoming off balance.

Over-wrap A type of tape used to cover the grip to absorb moisture and prevent slippage.

Racket face The entire string plane of the racket.

Racket head The entire string plane of the racket including the surrounding frame.

Rally When the ball is hit back and forth over the net.

Ready hop Refers to the slight "jump" that a player takes as an opponent is making contact with the ball. Sometimes referred to as a "split-step."

Ready position Refers to the stance that a player takes when awaiting the opponent's shot.

Semi-western grip The way the racket is held specifically for a topspin forehand.

Serve The overhead shot that starts every point and which must land within the opponent's service box.

Serve and volley Type of strategy where a player will serve and then immediately proceed to the net.

Service box Refers to any of the boxes that are formed from the lines on the court adjacent to the net, bounded by the baseline, center line, and sidelines.

Service line The line on the court that extends across the middle of the court between the singles sidelines.

Set The part of scoring when the total games needed to win a set is typically six, by a margin of two. Sometimes a set score will extend to seven if a special "tiebreaker" game is played, or if the margin of two is 7–5.

Singles sideline The lines on the side of the court at the inside of each alley.

Slice When a ball travels forward through the air while spinning underneath itself. Also referred to as "backspin." (May also mean "side spin" specifically on a serve.)

Split-step Refers to the slight "jump" that a player takes as an opponent is making contact with the ball. Sometimes referred to as a "ready hop."

Straight backswing A specific type of backswing when the racket is brought back straight behind the body in preparation for the forward swing.

Stretch racket Any racket length beyond the standard 27 inches (68.5 cm).

Sweet spot The part of the racket in the center of the strings.

Swing path The forward direction of the swing.

Swing speed The forward acceleration of the racket.

Tiebreaker A specific type of game when the set score reaches 6–6, using an alternate scoring system.

Topspin When a ball travels forward through the air while spinning over itself. Sometimes referred to as "overspin."

Toss The underhand throw of the ball in the air, which the player will use to serve to the opponent.

Touch shot The term used to describe any type of shot that requires soft contact between the racket and the ball.

Volley The shot where a player hits the ball before the bounce (usually occurs near the net).

Volley position A specific position of the body when preparing to hit a volley (sometimes refers to the location of the court near the net).

Western grip The way the racket is held specifically for a topspin forehand.

The Basics

It is assumed throughout this book that most of you reading have had enough experience playing tennis that a lot of preliminary information is unnecessary. However, common sense tells us that there are some basic issues that need to be addressed at any level of play. These include how to properly warm up and stretch, and how to know which type of equipment you should be using. Having a good awareness of both of these issues will be to your advantage when it comes to avoiding any type of injury, and being able to enjoy the game of tennis for years to come.

Warming up before starting any strenuous physical activity is extremely important in order to gradually raise the heart rate and initiate good blood circulation. It is also important to warm up before stretching. Many injuries occur because a player will overstretch a muscle when it is cold. A good warm-up consists of five to seven minutes of an activity such as jogging, jumping jacks, or jumping rope.

Remember to start off lightly and relax. I usually have players begin a slow rally from the service line in order to mimic the abbreviated motions of the tennis strokes that

Calf stretch

Hold onto the net in front of you and stretch out one leg behind you. Gradually press your weight toward the back of your heel until you feel the stretch in the back of the lower leg. Repeat two sets on each leg.

Quad stretch

With your back to the net, hold onto the net with both hands and lift one foot behind you, bending at the knee. Support your foot on the net as you lower yourself down into the stretch. Feel the stretch in the front of the upper leg. Stretch and hold for ten seconds and repeat this twice for each leg.

Hamstring stretch

Place the heel of your foot up on the net or at the end of a bench. Gradually extend your leg out without locking your knee. Lean forward and relax as you try to touch your ankle or your toes. Feel the stretch in the back of the mid and upper leg. Hold for ten seconds and repeat the stretch with the other leg.

Lower and mid-back stretch

Stretch your arms out to the side of you or hold your racket against your stomach. Twist slowly from side to side gradually extending your range of motion. Breathe deeply in and out toward the end of each turn. Repeat as necessary until your mid-section feels at ease.

will be used at the baseline. As long as players remember that the intent is to loosen up the body slightly, it is sufficient as a warm-up. You should feel that you are beginning to break a sweat. After a few minutes of hitting from the service line, a full set of stretches will precede the continuation of the warm-up from the baseline.

Stretching helps avoid injuries by elongating muscles gradually before peak output performance. Always relax and breathe into a stretched position. Brace yourself on either the net or a bench to give yourself balance. Hold each stretch comfortably for 10 seconds. Remember to stretch again after your practice or match. This is important because muscles tighten when they are fatigued and when air and body temperatures cool rapidly.

It is always a good idea to include some type of additional strength and endurance training beyond your tennis activity. Also remember to drink plenty of fluids to keep yourself hydrated, especially on hot or humid days. Dehydration can lead to muscle cramps and general fatigue. Always include proper rest and care for any extended injuries or chronic pain. Always check with a sports-injury physician if any pain persists.

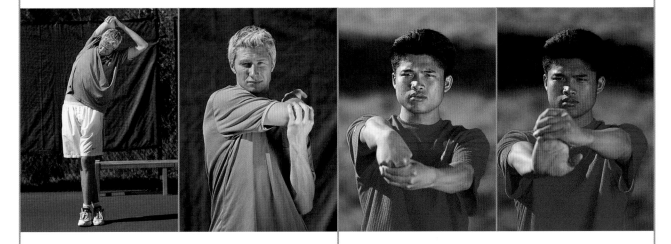

Shoulder and mid-back stretch

Bring your elbow up next to your head and gently pull it back behind your head with your other hand. This loosens out the lower part of the shoulder. Then slowly lean toward the opposite side as you feel a comfortable stretch in the side of your mid-back. Make sure to breathe into this part of the back during the stretch. Repeat twice on each side.

Shoulder and upper-back stretch

Bring your elbow across the front of your chest with your opposite hand as you feel a stretch across the outside of the shoulder and upper back. Hold for 10 seconds and repeat each side twice.

Wrist and forearm stretches

The most common injury occurring among tennis players is the dreaded "tennis elbow." This can arise from any number of reasons—overuse, improper technique, weak wrist and/or forearm muscles, poor equipment, or a combination of any of these—so it's very important to stretch out this area of the arm. Simply extend your arm out as much as possible and push your wrist down from the back of your hand. This stretches out the muscles on top of the forearm. Then take your opposite hand and pull your fingers back as you feel the stretch underneath the forearm. These should be repeated as often as three times a day if you are playing regularly. Remember to balance your routine by stretching the opposite arm as well.

Equipment

Just as exercise is vital to the prevention of injuries, choosing the proper equipment is important as well. I have seen players choose the wrong type of racket only to end up with tennis elbow a few weeks or a couple of months later. Some players complain of foot pain or knee pain as I look at their worn-out tennis shoes.

If you plan on enjoying the game of tennis for years to come you need to protect yourself from injuries by choosing good-quality rackets and shoes. This means that you may have to pay a little more, but this extra expense in both of these areas does make a difference.

Most standard adult rackets are 27 inches (68.5 cm) long. Recently, however, "stretch" rackets have come on the market. These rackets range from 27½ to 28½ inches (69.75 to 72.25 cm) long. The only obvious advantage to a stretch racket is that you have a bit more reach on your serve or your volley.

The size of the head of the racket can vary as well. These sizes are typically 95 square inches (237.5 sq cm)

for mid-size, 100 square inches (250 sq cm) for midplus, and 110 square inches (275 sq cm) for an oversize racket head. The exact sizes can vary somewhat. The advantage of a larger head size is that the sweet spot of the racket is bigger. The disadvantage is that it can seem more difficult to quickly maneuver the racket into position to hit the ball. Most pros play with smaller-size racket heads and most recreational players choose oversize rackets.

The thickness of the racket is important, too. Generally, the thicker the racket, the stiffer it is (less flex when you hit it). A stiffer racket means that the ball pops off the racket quickly. A player who has a long swing path or a fast swing speed should choose a thinner frame. This has a direct relation to the weight of the racket as well.

Recent advances in racket-frame materials have produced lighter and stronger rackets than ever before, but this can have a downside. It is getting to the point where many players are buying rackets because they feel

nice and light and they are easy to swing. However, this results in players having a harder time controlling their shots. It doesn't matter how fast you can swing a pencil, for example, it still won't have enough weight in it to reverse the direction of a speeding train. Well, I think you at least get the idea.

The size of the grip on the racket is an important aspect as well. Most grip sizes are between 4¼ and 4¾ inches (11.25 and 11.875 cm). The rule to follow when determining the correct grip size for you is to wrap your hand around the grip. You should be able to fit the width of your index finger comfortably between the thumb and two middle fingers. It is better to have too large a grip than too small a grip. However, you can always make your grip bigger with overwrap tape or shrink tubing if you need to, but you can't make it any smaller.

The strings in the racket make a huge difference in the way the racket plays and feels. Most pros play with natural gut, which is very expensive. Recreational players have a wide variety of good quality, relatively inexpensive synthetic strings to choose from. A multi-filament string is a good choice for most players because it has a "softer" feel at contact and is easier on the arm. Generally, a racket is strung with 55–65 lb. of tension. This depends on the manufacturer's recommendation for the racket. The tighter the racket is strung, the more control you will

have, and the looser the racket is strung, the more power the racket will feel like it has. If you are having some pain in the arm it is a good idea to string your racket at a lower tension. If you are losing control of your shots very often, try to string the racket a little tighter. The thickness of the string can make a difference in the amount of control you have as well. A 16-gauge string is pretty standard for most players. However, a thinner string such as a 17- or 18-gauge will allow the string to penetrate, or "bite" into the ball more, which can add to your control. The only disadvantage of a thinner string is that it is more likely to break or wear out sooner.

From all of this information, you should be able to draw conclusions for yourself as to which type of racket will fit into your level and style of play. One racket isn't necessarily better than another. If it were, then everyone would be using it.

The most important advice I can give if you are thinking about changing rackets is to play with at least five or six and compare the way they feel. Everyone has different opinions. Many retail stores and pro shops will let you try out rackets before you buy. My other advice is to do yourself a favor and buy good-quality equipment. From rackets, to shoes, to sun protection, it can really make a difference between having fun and being miserable—both on and off the court.

Grips Section

There is quite a variety of different ways to hold a tennis racket. It is very important to have a good understanding of how you can use these various grips to your best advantage.

Basically, a grip determines how the racket face will be angled at the point of contact with the ball. This depends upon the position of the wrist as well. However, using the proper grip should allow the wrist to be in a comfortable and stable position at the contact point. This will allow more consistent ball contact with the sweet spot of the racket. This is an extremely important aspect of hitting a tennis ball effectively.

Eastern forehand grip

BELOW **The panels of the racket handle.**

LEFT HANDED PLAYER   RIGHT HANDED PLAYER

Top panel   Top panel

Top angled panel   Top angled panel

Side panel   Side panel

Bottom angled panel   Bottom angled panel

BELOW **Heel of the hand, opposite side of the thumb.**

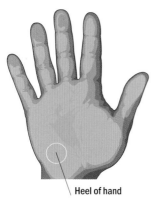

Heel of hand

The grip most widely used by recreational players is called the eastern forehand grip. This places the heel of the hand directly on the side panel. Some people refer to this as the "shake hands" grip. The racket face basically becomes an extension of the arm because it puts the strings at the same angle as the palm of the hand. This grip is used effectively on forehand groundstrokes with or without topspin. Many recreational players become well accustomed to this grip and continue to use it on other shots as well. Although it is easy to use on a serve or forehand volley, it is not as effective as the appropriate change of grip for variations of these shots. All professional tennis players will change their grips for serves and volleys, as well as for many other types of shots.

Our discussion here will involve what these grips look like and what they feel like. It is important to be able to "feel" the proper grip, because in the middle of the point you cannot call time out to see if you are holding the proper grip for the next shot. Throughout the book we will refer back to this section on grips in order for you to fully understand which grips are best for which shots, and which ones will not work on a particular shot.

The most effective way to determine how a grip should feel is by referencing the palm of the hand with the various panels of the racket handle. Specifically, the heel of the hand on the opposite side of the thumb is used to sense where the hand is to be positioned on the grip or as it's also called, the racket handle.

Understanding the various grips and being able to use them appropriately is very important to your tennis

Western forehand grip

Eastern backhand grip

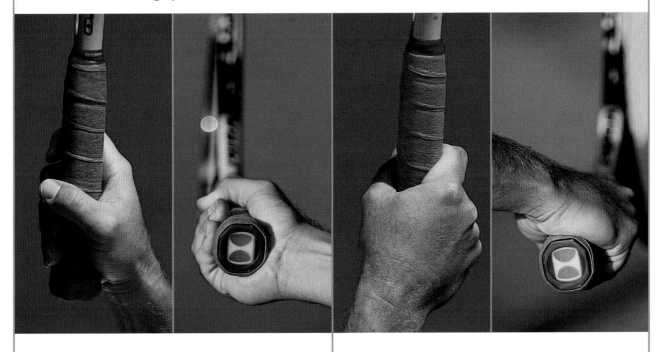

Two other grips that are being used by top juniors and professional players are the "semi-western" and "western" forehand grips. These grips are similar to each other. They basically place the hand further underneath the racket handle. The heel of the hand will line up with the bottom angled panel. This "closes" the racket face, or turns it more toward the ground. An "open" racket face tilts the strings upward toward the sky. A "flat" racket face is straight up and down, perpendicular to the ground. Swinging the racket with a closed face can impart a great deal of topspin to the ball. The western and semi-western grips can be used effectively only for forehand topspin groundstrokes. A western grip simply places the hand further underneath the racket handle than the semi-western grip.

The backhand groundstroke uses one of two grips. I have not heard much distinction between the two, but there is a definite difference. The first backhand grip is called the "eastern backhand" grip. It is used mostly for slice backhands. This grip places the heel of the hand on the top panel and this creates a slightly "open" racket face as contact is made.

development. Using the wrong grip will not allow your body to understand how to hit the ball correctly, and it could lead to an injury as well. It is also very important to have your non-dominant hand on the racket after you hit each shot as you return to the ready position. The non-dominant hand will assist with the grip changes by twisting the racket as swing preparation occurs.

Another important question to answer is, "What grip should I have in the ready position?" At the baseline you should have whatever grip you will use most often on your forehand groundstroke. This is because you will hit more forehands off a serve than you will backhands. If

the ball comes directly toward you at the baseline, you should move to the side where you will hit a forehand groundstroke. At the net, you should be prepared with the hammer grip. This allows you to get the racket face into a quick volley position if the ball is coming at you very quickly.

Pay close attention to which grips you are currently using on all of your shots. Practice changing your grip appropriately for each shot, and try to become aware of feeling the different grips without looking at them. A solid understanding of the various grips can improve a player's game drastically.

| Extreme backhand grip | Hammer grip |

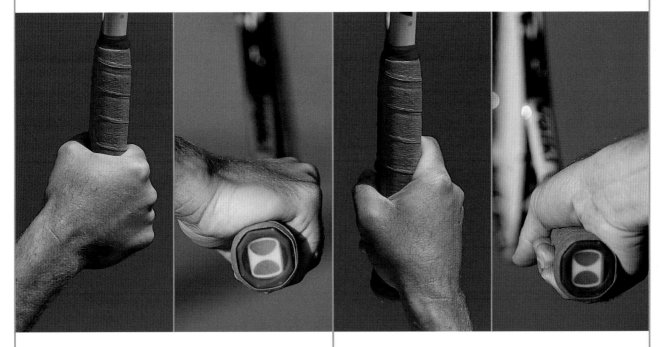

The other backhand grip is used more for a topspin groundstroke. It is called the "extreme" backhand grip. The heel of the hand positions slightly past the top panel and the entire hand has now formed a fist on the racket. The front knuckles of the fist are parallel with the strings of the racket. This grip requires good wrist and forearm muscles to provide support at the contact point of the swing.

LEFT **Sergei Bruguera of Spain playing a forehand shot with a western grip.**

The final grip to learn is called the "hammer" grip. This grip is also commonly called the "continental" grip. I prefer the name "hammer" grip because it describes how the racket should be held, like a hammer. The heel of the hand is placed on the end of the racket where the top panel meets the angled panel. You will learn to feel a knob directly on the end of the racket where it flares out. This grip is used on many different shots in tennis but the main uses are serves, volleys, lobs, overhead smash, and drop shots. Some players will actually use this grip rather effectively on every shot. It does not work well on high-bouncing groundstrokes unless you are attempting to slice the ball with backspin.

CHAPTER ONE

Stroke Production Skills

Good fundamental skills provide the framework for success in any sport. Tennis is no exception. This chapter will provide information to help you acquire the basic skills that support this framework.

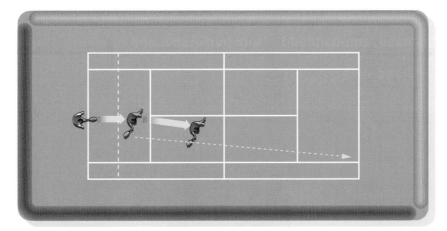

The approach shot— *see page* 48

To hit a tennis ball effectively you must have your body positioned correctly in relation to the ball at the point of contact. In other words, you need to be standing in the right place when you swing. A picture-perfect swing will not do much good if it doesn't swing through the path of the ball. For the sake of this chapter, it should be understood that the descriptions provided for stroke development will assume that a player is standing in the right place.

On the other hand, perfect position will not be much help if an improper swing is being used. Each of these principles goes hand in hand. Therefore, Chapter 1 will discuss some of the basic concepts of the skills necessary to achieve proper stroke production for a variety of shots. Footwork skills and drills will be covered in a later chapter.

One of the most effective ways to improve stroke production skills is with a ball machine. This keeps the ball in a consistent contact location so the necessary swing development can occur. If a ball machine is not available, have a coach or your practice partner feed you balls in the same location. This practice will create a rhythm and establish good timing.

Groundstrokes

Groundstrokes are the foundation of a tennis player's skills. There are many different ways to hit a tennis ball, and with various amounts of speed and spin. This section will focus on the basic elements of four different shots—topspin forehand, two-handed backhand, one-handed topspin backhand, and one-handed backhand slice.

1 **2** **3** **4**

Preparation for the swing begins from the ready position (1) with a turn of the shoulders and a high racket position (2).

This high racket preparation is deceiving because the racket head must drop well below the contact point in order to create the "scraping" effect needed to generate topspin on the ball (3 and 4). The reason that the racket starts higher is so that a looping type of backswing generates enough racket acceleration to put spin on the ball. If you are trying to hit topspin for the first time, you may need to avoid the higher backswing until you get the feel of the spin.

TOP **The wrist position remains in a fixed position that is bent backwards slightly, this allows for a contact point forward of the hip.**

FOREHAND

The first type of groundstroke we will discuss is the forehand. The forehand groundstroke is usually a player's strongest shot. Today's players are hitting the ball much harder mainly because of recent advancements in racket technology. This, combined with widespread play on hard court and clay court surfaces where the ball bounces higher, has encouraged most players to hit groundshots with "topspin." This overspinning effect allows for more control because the ball can be hit higher above the net and it will still come down into the court because of the diving effect created by topspin. This type of spin on the ball generates a sudden "kick" after it has bounced on these types of surfaces.

Contacting the ball at a higher point off the ground and creating spin requires the use of the "semi-western grip." This grip allows the racket face to close over the top of the ball as contact is made. An eastern forehand grip can be used to generate topspin on the ball as well, but closing the racket face with the western or semi-western grips allows for more freedom of the wrist and forearm, which allows for quicker acceleration of the racket head.

5   6   7   8

The contact point is higher and the racket face has a scraping effect as it swings up the back of the ball (5 and 6). Also notice the forward point of contact with the wrist bent, and the openness of the stance. This allows for quick acceleration using the hips, and quicker movements toward the ball and during recovery.

With its continuation and the follow-through more toward the side, the swing has a windshield-wiper action (7 and 8) and the elbow finishes out in front of the chin.

RIGHT **The wrist remains firm as the forearm rotates 180 degrees. This forearm rotation accelerates the racket head up, over, and across the ball.**

TWO-HANDED BACKHAND

The backhand groundstroke is usually hit one of three ways. If one hand is used during the swing, a player will hit the ball with either topspin or backspin (slice). If two hands are used for the backhand, topspin is generally used on this shot. Trying to put backspin on the ball using two hands is uncommon and very difficult to achieve. There has been a lot of discussion as to which backhand is the more advantageous: one-handed or two. Players who use a two-handed backhand will usually have a stronger return of serve. However, players who hit two-handed backhands will usually have a harder time hitting backhand volleys effectively because they are so used to holding the racket with two hands.

The first concept to understand about the two-handed backhand is that you will actually be using the non-dominant arm (your left if you're right-handed) to do

1

2

3

Most students don't seem to have any problems with the proper grip when they hit the backhand with two hands. From the photo sequence you can see that this player has gone from the ready position immediately to the shoulder turn and backswing (1 and 2). Also notice in this position that the knees are bent and the body is extremely coiled from the hips through the shoulders.

The swing begins with a small forward step, or weight transfer, as the racket head drops below the contact point (3). Remember that, as with the forehand topspin swing, the racket face must scrape the back of the ball from bottom to top in order to lift it slightly and impart the overspin on the ball.

ABOVE **Here the right hand is using a backhand grip.**

▲ **MASTER STROKE** ▲

Adult beginners and junior players seem to have more success with the two-handed backhand. This is because it is easier to generate force on the swing with two arms, and holding the racket with two hands helps to stabilize the racket face on off-center hits.

most of the work for you. Think of using a topspin forehand swing with your non-dominant hand and simply add your dominant hand at the bottom of the racket for control. The non-dominant hand should hold the racket with the eastern forehand grip. The dominant hand, at the bottom of the grip, can hold the racket whichever way feels most comfortable. This is usually an eastern backhand grip, or a hammer grip (see page 15).

4   **5**   **6**

Contact (4) is at about waist level. The arms are extended but the elbows are bent comfortably. Notice that the knees have straightened more as the swing progresses through its full motion. This establishes good balance during the swing and enhances the low to high swing path.

Continuation of the contact takes the racket over the top of the ball and slightly across it as well (5).This is one advantage of having two hands on the racket (see inset photo 4). Both hands will allow for better use of the wrists when trying to scrape the ball. This can also deceive the opponent because a quick snap of the wrists can quickly change the direction of the shot.

The follow-through should take the racket all the way up around the back of the head as the chest ends up facing the net (6).

> ### ▲ MASTER STROKE ▲
> There will be certain balls that a two-handed backhand won't be able to reach, such as very wide balls at the baseline and very low balls that land short in the court. The best situation would be to learn all three types of backhands. Unfortunately, they are all very different and most players will choose one or the other.
> My suggestion is to attempt each of the backhands and try to determine which ones feel the most natural to your style and development.

ONE-HANDED BACKHAND

The one-handed topspin backhand has a similar low to high swing path as the two-handed shot, but it is executed with only one hand. Most recreational players have difficulty with this shot because it takes perfect position and timing, and enough wrist and forearm strength to generate sufficient racket speed to hit the ball with a lot of spin. Nevertheless, this type of one-handed backhand swing can be an effective shot when even a small amount of spin is applied.

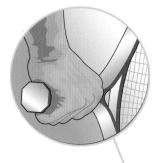

1　　**2**　　**3**　　**4**

The one-handed backhand begins with the usual turn of the shoulders and early racket preparation (1 and 2). There is a very important change to make as you turn from the ready position into the backswing: you have to use an extreme backhand grip in order to hit a one-handed topspin backhand. This means that the back of the hand comes over the top of the grip and the front of the fist is parallel with the strings of the racket (see inset on photo 5 and Grips page 14). The non-dominant hand assists with this grip change by turning the racket as the grip is changed. This grip change allows the wrist to be in a firm but comfortable position at the contact point with the racket positioned straight up and down.

Notice from the photo sequence that the racket head has dropped very low and the knees are bent as well (3 and 4). This player is stepping in toward the net to generate force from the transfer of the body weight. Much of the force to hit the ball comes from the uncoiling of the shoulders.

▲ MASTER STROKE ▲

Students seem to have more success with this shot if they turn and position the racket low in the backswing. Remember that the racket head must drop below the contact point anyway, and the preparation for this type of backhand takes longer than any other shot from the baseline. It saves time to position the racket head low right away. It is also very important that you hold the racket on the throat with the non-dominant hand until the racket has begun to swing forward. The non-dominant hand helps to stabilize the racket in the backswing. It becomes very difficult to swing backward and then quickly forward using only one arm.

5   **6**   **7**

As contact is made (5), the weight has transferred from the ground up into the hips and finally into the shoulders through the point of contact. The contact height is about waist level with the ball comfortably forward of the body. The racket arm is extended but not locked at the elbow. A common error on the one-handed backhand occurs after contact is made and the shoulders continue to rotate too far. This will very often bring the racket face away from the contact point too soon, causing numerous errors.

The follow-through on the one-handed backhand is more forward and up, and the chest remains to the side (6 and 7). You can also see from the photos that this follow-through is quite different than the two-handed backhand.

SLICE BACKHAND

The one-handed slice backhand is a very common shot and is fairly easy to accomplish. This shot attempts to impart backspin or underspin on the ball. Slice, backspin, and underspin all basically mean the same thing. This shot is not usually used as an offensive shot.

However, proper shot placement and good control of the spin can make this a difficult shot for your opponent.

When a ball bounces with backspin it either skips quickly across the court surface if it is hit low and hard, or, if it is lofted up higher, it tends to float through the air

From the ready position (1) the shoulders turn as usual, and the non-dominant hand helps position the racket in the backswing with the fingers holding the throat of the racket (2). A slight grip change occurs as it did in the previous description of the one-handed backhand. However, since the racket face will be slightly upward, or "open," at the contact point, the hand should rotate only a little bit over the top of the racket (see inset photo 3). A very slight adjustment in the grip can bring on big changes at the contact point.

Notice from the sequence of photos that the backswing is fairly high at this point. It doesn't take as long to set up for the slice backhand because the shoulders don't have to go back as far. The reason for this is that the ball will carry on under its own momentum when it has backspin. Hitting the ball too hard on this shot makes the ball sail past the baseline. The backswing can be fairly short. It is also important that the swing motion begin with a forward step that will transfer weight into the contact point (3).

and then sort of stops as it bounces off the ground. This is why if a drop shot is hit with backspin, the ball tends to die after it bounces.

The swing path for the slice backhand is much different than any of the other groundstrokes we have discussed so far. In order to generate the backspin, the ball must be contacted from high to low and the racket face is slightly open as it scratches the ball. Therefore, the swing path is from high to low, or somewhat level if the point of contact is down below the waist.

4   5   6

The contact point is slightly to the side of the body (4) and not as far forward as the one-handed topspin swing. When contact is properly done, it should feel a bit like a punching motion.

The racket face then continues to drag beneath the ball as it scrapes the bottom of the ball (5). This creates the backspin. The follow-through remains out in front as it chases the ball when it has left the racket. The chest is facing the side as this shot is completed (6).

▲ MASTER STROKE ▲

Experiment with the grip on the slice backhand in order to get the right feel of the shot. If the ball continues to pop up in the air upon contact—a common problem—adjust the grip so the racket faces more straight up and down, or "flat," at the contact point. Leave the opposite hand on the throat of the racket until the forward part of the swing is well under way.

Volleys

In order to develop an effective volley, players must remember that they have to spend a good amount of time playing at the net. Many students have spent most of their time on a tennis court continuing to play out practice rallies from the baseline—many times even hitting the ball after it bounces twice on their side of the net. As a result, their groundstrokes are getting pretty good, but they never develop an adequate volley.

FOREHAND VOLLEY

The first element of a successful volley is to be at ease using the "hammer" grip. It is called the hammer grip because it feels much as if you were holding a hammer with the edge of the racket striking the nail. It is also called the "continental" grip because it was used in the past on European grass courts. Although it is necessary to become familiar with what the grip should look like, you will not have time in the middle of a point to look down at your racket and see if it is correct. You must be able to feel that you have the correct hand position (see page 15).

The hammer grip is used on a variety of shots. Some recreational players will try to use an eastern forehand grip on a volley. This will work pretty well when the ball is contacted above the height of the net, but when the ball gets down around the ankles it becomes very difficult and awkward to try to lift the ball up over the net. Give the hammer grip a chance: it will become very valuable on other shots, including the serve and the overhead smash.

1

When standing near the net in the ready position (1), you should be prepared with the hammer grip (see inset). Being close to the net doesn't allow enough time to be changing the grip all of the time. This is why the hammer grip is so important. It allows you to hit the ball on either side of your body without changing the grip. A good point of contact for a volley is at shoulder height. This allows for good position and balance, the use of body weight as a counterforce, and a good margin of error above the net. Therefore, in the ready position at the net, the head of the racket should be held up a bit more than in the ready position at the baseline.

2

▼ FAULT FINDER ▼

The most common mistake on a volley is that the player brings the racket back too far in preparation for the shot. This results in a swinging motion where the ball is being hit too late, or too hard. This also makes it difficult to hit the ball consistently on the sweet spot of the racket. Once the volley position is established, proper footwork should place the body in the most comfortable hitting position. One of the most prolific volleyers in tennis was Stefan Edberg, who used to say that he would volley with his feet. Which meant that, if he could move his body into a comfortable hitting position, he could make a comfortable and efficient volley. This is why staying on your toes, literally, is so important.

A good "volley position" should now be established (2). Our first discussion involves the forehand volley. The volley position is critical because it sets the arm and shoulders in preparation for contact.

▲ MASTER STROKE ▲

As soon as the ball leaves the opponent's racket you will need to get into the volley position. This begins with a shoulder turn left or right depending on the location of the oncoming ball. Your mind has to react quickly to determine if it is a forehand or a backhand volley. This quick decision is many times the most difficult part of the volley. Practicing the volley drills described in Chapter 3 will allow you to become more comfortable with these quick responses.

3   **4**   **5**

Once the correct volley position is located, a precisely timed step forward to the ball, just prior to contact, will allow sufficient body weight to counteract the force of the oncoming ball (3). This is provided that there is enough time to do so. Contact is made out in front of the body and toward the net (4).

Try not to straighten out the arm completely at contact, because this will not allow sufficient use of the body weight to occur. The elbow should be bent slightly at contact so that some of the upper arm and shoulder muscles can be used. When contact is made at shoulder height, the forward "punching" motion should be made from a slightly high to low position, and with a moderately open racket face. As contact continues, the racket face begins to slide underneath the ball in order to control the ball effectively (5). This slight wrist rotation curls the racket face underneath the ball as it leaves

contact with the racket (see inset photo 6). The ball may start to spin backward as a result. What this spin actually does is keep the ball on the face of the strings for a fraction of a second longer, almost "holding" it on the racket long enough for the player to better control the placement of the shot as it leaves the strings.

Be careful with the concept here: although backspin is good because it keeps the ball low after the bounce, it is not the goal. The goal is to control the ball. Trying to "chop" the ball is a common mistake of recreational players. This chopping motion will bring the racket face to the ball at such an acute angle that it will be difficult to make contact consistently on the sweet spot of the racket. Try to keep the forward motion of the arm short, simple, and at the same level of the ball. "Less is more," and it will allow for a quicker recovery for the next shot.

6

The follow-through should be rather short, and the racket face should chase the ball as it leaves the strings of the racket (6). The slower the ball is coming toward you the more pronounced your follow-through should be. Balls that are hit to you at a faster pace should be hit with more of a "blocking" motion.

RIGHT **Great Britain's Men's Singles hope, Tim Henman, Wimbledon 1999, going for a difficult wide volley.**

BACKHAND VOLLEY

A backhand volley follows many of the principles of the forehand volley, such as early preparation, positioning the body using solid footwork, and moving forward at the point of contact. One important point is that the backhand volley should be used more often than the forehand. This is because it is quicker to prepare the racket in the backhand position than the forehand position if the ball is coming directly at the body.

1

2

3

In the backhand volley sequence of photos above, you will see the non-dominant hand stabilizing the racket in the volley position (see inset photo 2). The opposite hand will help to position the racket more effectively than trying to use one hand only. When the forward step is made toward the ball,

however, the dominant hand will take the racket out of the opposite hand to make contact with the ball. The opposite hand is then used to maintain balance.

While we are discussing proper technique used for the backhand volley, it should be pointed out that many

▲ **MASTER STROKE** ▲

A backhand volley will be easier to hit with a grip change to the backhand side. At higher levels of play where the players are hitting the ball at faster speeds, there isn't enough time to adjust the grip at the net. However, at a recreational level, which most of us are more accustomed to, we have a bit more time to allow for the change. Practice the backhand volley with and without the change of grip. The time to change the grip is between the ready position and the volley position. As the shoulders turn in preparation for the shot, the opposite hand will guide this slight twist of the racket. This is one reason why it is so important to have the non-dominant hand cradling the throat of the racket with the fingers.

4

5

6

recreational players will try to use two hands to hit a backhand volley. These are usually the same players that hit a two-handed backhand groundstroke from the baseline. Once again, at the professional level we don't see any players using a two-handed volley. At the recreational level, it is being used with limited success. The main disadvantages are the limited reach to the ball with both hands on the racket, inadequacy on low balls, and difficulty maneuvering the racket in front of the body. The best solution would be to take the extra time to practice the one-handed backhand volley, following the guidelines in this book.

LOW FOREHAND VOLLEY

It should be pointed out that the descriptions given so far have assumed that the contact point is at a comfortable position at about shoulder height. However, many balls will be volleyed from a height below the waist, and a slightly different technique should be used.

The most common mistake that I see players make when trying to hit a low volley is that the head doesn't follow the ball down into the racket. This usually results from the legs not getting the body down low enough to the ball (see above).

Above you can see how the player has the back leg bent to the point where the knee is almost touching the ground. This low position enables the player to keep good balance, and it allows him to position the racket parallel with the ground so that the face of the racket can be more controllable with a slight movement of the wrist. In general, the lower the contact point of the volley, the more tilted, or "open," the racket face should be. Nothing but the hammer grip will allow this proper contact position to occur. Be careful not to swing at the ball. A low volley is a defensive shot that needs to be hit with a short blocking motion. In most cases, the racket should not move forward into the ball more than about a foot (30 cm).

HIGH FOREHAND VOLLEY

A high volley is a ball that is up above your head, but not quite high enough to take a full overhead smash type of swing. The most common error that occurs on this ball is that players attempt to produce a full swing when it is unnecessary.

BLOCK VOLLEY

A "block volley" is a ball that is hit right at the body without the player having the time to turn the shoulders into a good volley position. A backhand volley should be used because, although feeling awkward, it is the quickest way to respond to the shot and be able to position the racket well enough in the path of the ball.

The most important thing to remember is that you must keep the face of the racket in the path of the ball. Prepare the arms quickly as if it were going to be an overhead smash, then snap the racket face down on top of the ball using mostly wrist and forearm to ensure good solid contact. Speed will be generated from ball contact on the center of the strings, and good leverage from the legs. Proper placement of the shot is still the key to winning the point on a volley.

Above are examples of block volleys at the waist, and at the face. The elbow of the racket arm pulls outward while the face of the racket becomes square to the ball.

There is no time to change the grip on this shot. When playing at the net you should have a hammer grip in the ready position. Squeeze the racket tight at the contact point, and try to punch forward using the wrist and forearm only. Once again it is very important to keep the face of the racket in the path of the ball.

In the case of the block volley at the face (see above right) it is a good idea to lean away from the ball as contact is made, otherwise it might end up being your face getting in the path of the ball.

Serve

A good serve in tennis is essential. Every point in a tennis match begins with a serve. Probably the most analyzed shot in tennis, an effective serve requires precise timing and arm coordination.

Most recreational players don't have much trouble just getting the ball into the service box. However, most students complain about the "cream puff" that usually results from their serve. While we would all like to serve rockets like the pros, we have to keep things in perspective. There are other ways to develop an effective serve without blasting the ball every time. Stan Smith once said that having a successful serve requires variety. This involves placement, spin, speed, and various combinations of all three.

Not all of the principles that I will discuss in this section may apply to what you are doing incorrectly on your serve. The final thing to keep in mind is that, by trying to change one element of the serve, it will usually have an effect on another part of the serve. For instance, by attempting to use more of a backswing to add some speed to the serve, you will need to toss the ball higher. Your timing will change because you are adding an additional motion to the serve.

While the serve is a complicated motion, the following descriptions are short and simple. The serve can be divided into two phases: the preparation phase, which involves the stance, grip, and toss; and the swing phase.

LEFT John McEnroe would stand with his feet almost parallel to the baseline to the point where his back was facing the opponent. We all know what a great serve he had, however, this doesn't mean that you need to stand the same way.

The grip used for the serve is the hammer grip (see page 15). Of all the difficulties that players have with the serve, it is usually with either the grip or the toss that problems originate. If an improper grip is used for the serve, development is limited. Many recreational players serve with the eastern forehand grip. This grip forces a player to use mostly the arm on the serve. As a result, direction is easily achieved, but speed and spin are never developed. An effective serve requires a complete use of the entire body working together in a chain reaction. The end result at the contact point requires the use of the hammer grip to facilitate this chain reaction.

1   2   3

The only requirement of a proper stance is that you are turned sideways enough to allow for the rotation of the shoulders to occur during the swing. Precisely locating the feet along the baseline is only a matter of personal preference. Whatever stance you choose, you will need to relax and feel that you have good balance to begin the serve motions. Taking a deep breath while bouncing the ball a couple of times will help you relax and focus. The toss begins with both the racket and tossing arm out in front of the body (1).

The ball should be held in the hand with the palm facing up (see inset). To make the initial motion simple, try to think of both arms going down together, then up together (2) although from the third and fourth photograph of this sequence (see next page), you will notice that this player has developed a personal style of leaving the racket arm down until later in the motion. This technique is more difficult to accomplish but can provide greater racket acceleration.

THE BALL TOSS

The toss of the ball for a flat serve (without spin) should be high enough to allow time for all of the necessary body motions to occur, and a full extension of the arm at the contact point. The ball should be contacted as it is falling down from its peak. The location of the toss for a flat serve should be out into the court slightly enough to allow forward momentum to occur on the swing and good leverage using the legs. The forward toss also allows the racket face to snap down over the top of the ball at the contact point. Hitting the ball too deep or too

4   **5**   **6**

As the ball is released from the hand the knees start to bend and the tossing arm remains completely extended at the side of the head. The swinging arm bends at the elbow and positions the racket somewhere behind the back of the head. You should also arch your back and attempt to coil your body and reverse your shoulders as much as possible. This will allow for maximum range of motion necessary to generate force during the swing phase. This concludes the preparation phase of the serve.

Once the ball reaches the top of the toss, the body begins to uncoil as the ball starts to drop from its peak. In photo 6 you can see that the left arm has begun to drop from the elbow and the shoulders have spread out to their maximum range of motion across the chest. It is important to hold the right shoulder back until the last instant in order to achieve maximum acceleration from the forward shoulder turn. The final link involves the precise mechanics of the arm and wrist. It is not easy to control all of the energy that is produced and high is a common result of not tossing the ball far enough forward. A good experiment to practice the location of the toss is to let the ball drop and see where it lands on the ground. A good toss should fall about 1 or 2 feet (30–60 centimeters) in front of the foot that's closer to the baseline.

▲ MASTER STROKE ▲

The precise timing of the swing phase demands that the toss is going to be in the right location to contact it properly. Although the entire swing phase takes less than a second, the parts of the body must work in conjunction with each other to generate extreme force at the contact point. This sequence starts from the ground up by pushing forward and upward with the legs and shifting the weight from the back foot to the toes of the front foot at contact. While the legs are doing their part to shift the weight properly, the shoulders and torso take over this weight shift by transferring the energy from the legs up into the shoulders and arms.

produced and transferred into the acceleration of the swing. All of this energy should be thrown upward into the top of the racket as the wrist snaps forward to continue this extreme force and help control the ball as well. If the motion is done properly, it should feel like you are using a throwing motion while cracking a whip at the contact point.

COACH'S COMMENT

"The serve is an essential part of the game, and it is also the shot least practiced. Improving all aspects of the serve comes with practice. Pete Sampras' legendary serves may not be possible for all of us, but positive thinking and dedicated practice can ensure that your serves hit the spot every time."

GEORGE ZAHORSKY – USPTA Coaching Professional
Lagunitas Country Club
Ross, California

CONTACT ZONE

Now getting back to the hammer grip, you should notice that the only way to get a full motion from the snap of the wrist is to rotate the forearm outward during the swing. Notice from the photo sequence that, just prior to contact, through the continuation, the arm suddenly turns outward, or "pronates," through the contact zone. This can be performed only with the hammer grip. As

contact is made, the racket face squares up directly behind the ball. This causes a slapping effect that produces little or no spin on the ball.

The less spin on the ball, the faster it travels through the air. The only problem now is that the ball can clear the top of the net by no more than about a foot. Keep practicing!

In the sequence above, notice that this player has followed through on the serve by landing on his left foot. More and more professional players have been using this technique. This advanced technique is established because of the extreme upward force of the body that has been generated

from the legs. A baseline player can establish position quickly because the feet do not end up crossing over. Although we would all like to copy the pros, I would still recommend using the traditional forward motion where you end the serve on your dominant foot.

SPIN SERVE

Spin is produced by "scraping" the ball as you would on a topspin groundstroke. Using the hammer grip will position the racket face at an angle where the ball can be chopped, or "cut in half," without the outward rolling motion, or "pronation," of the arm.

As the wrist snaps, it scratches the racket face up across the back of the ball and finishes by coming around the top side of the ball. If you were to look at the ball as if it were a clock, you make contact with it at around two o'clock (see diagram below). Different variations of spin can be achieved with a little experimentation at the contact point. Try scratching the ball across the back starting from around seven o'clock and finishing around one o'clock. You will need to toss the ball further back and a bit more over your head than as described for the flat serve. This allows the racket face to come in contact with more of the ball as you strike it and creates more of a topspin effect on the ball. With practice, it can be further enhanced by use of the eastern backhand grip.

Trying to improve the serve can become a frustrating experience. Remember that attempting to change one aspect of the serve can have altering effects on another part of the swing. Experimentation is important. Be willing to make a lot of mistakes while you practice. Try not to "practice" your new serve technique during a match until you have gained confidence with it. You don't need a partner to practice your serve, just a basket or bag of used tennis balls.

There is another way to serve the ball: hit it with spin. Putting spin on the ball increases the margin for error because the ball can be hit higher over the net. The spin will make the ball curve downward and slightly to the side, depending on the angle of contact with the racket face. Spinning the ball won't make it go faster, but after it bounces in the service box it will jump off of the ground and cause problems for your opponent. Various combinations of spin and speed can add even more variation to your serve and keep your opponent off balance on the receiving end.

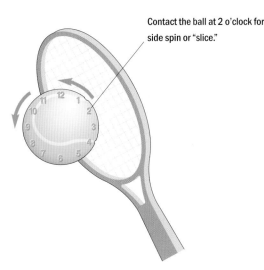

Contact the ball at 2 o'clock for side spin or "slice."

LEFT Australian star Pat Rafter serving in the 1999 Ausralian Open at Melbourne Park.

The drills later in this book will help provide a guideline for your practice sessions. These include "Serve Targets" on page 68, "Serve and Volley" on page 84, and "Invisible Man" on page 115.

Lob

A lob is a shot that is most often used in a defensive situation. It is usually hit from an area deep behind the baseline when a player is in trouble and on the run.

Hitting a good high lob deep into the opponent's court will allow you enough time to get out of trouble and get back into a good ready position to continue the point. Many times a good lob will turn a defensive situation into an offensive situation. A lob can also be useful as an offensive shot by attempting to hit the ball just out of the opponent's reach when they are at the net. This offensive lob attempt is made in an effort to win the point by not allowing the opponent enough time to run back to the baseline and return it. At the professional level, players will also add topspin to the ball to make it come down quicker after it has passed over the net player's head. A good lob is a necessity for a well-rounded player.

1

To hit a forehand lob, start by moving toward the ball while preparing the racket early (1). This means that the racket head should start from a very low position with the face of the strings tilted upward. It will be important to drop the racket head early so that the swing path begins almost directly below the ball.

▲ MASTER STROKE ▲

Many recreational players who use a loop backswing on their groundstrokes continue to use it when hitting a lob. As a result, the majority of lobs don't get high enough into the air. In order to hit the ball comfortably from underneath, the contact point needs to be near waist height or slightly higher. The grip used for a forehand lob should be either the hammer grip or the forehand grip (see Grips page 14).

2

3

The lob is what is known as a "touch shot," (2) which means that it is a control shot. A short backswing combined with a slower swing speed will allow for this softer contact. The racket face should be fairly "open" at contact.

The follow-through is the part of the swing that helps direct the ball just as contact with the ball is ending. This is crucial on all shots, especially the lob (3). A long and high follow-through will allow the ball to carry over the opponent's head and land deep into the court while contacting the ball softly enough to keep it under control.

▼ FAULT FINDER ▼

Often, a player who has an excessive backswing will stop the swing immediately after contact is made. This is because they realize that they will hit the ball too hard if they don't try to stop the swing, or at least slow it down. This causes the ball to shoot off in other directions because there is no follow-through to "carry" the ball on the strings of the racket.

BACKHAND LOB

Another tip concerning the one-hand backhand lob is to try to make sure that you are far enough away from the ball when beginning the swing. You really need a full swing to include a long follow-through. Crowding the ball will not allow any extension of the arm during the contact point or follow-through.

The backhand lob can be hit with either one hand or two hands on the racket. A one-handed backhand lob is much like the forehand lob in that the racket head begins well below the ball (1) with comfortable contact (2) being made above the waist, but not higher than the head. The grip used for the backhand lob is either the hammer grip or the eastern backhand grip. (See Grips page 14)

Once again, the follow-through (3) is extremely important, especially on the backhand side, because for many players it is difficult to generate enough force to hit the ball high enough with one hand.

TWO-HANDED BACKHAND LOB

The lob is very similar to a normal groundstroke swing, except that the swing path is more low to high and the racket face is more open, or "tilted upward," at contact point.

1 **2** **3**

A two-handed backhand shot really uses the force of the non-dominant hand to hit the ball. Therefore, it should be somewhat easier when using two hands, right? The advantages of the two-handed backhand lob are that you have a little more strength on the shot and you can quickly maneuver the racket using the wrists when you are in a hurry to get to the ball. The only disadvantage is that you don't have as much reach for the ball at the last second when you realize that you are not going to be close enough to hit it comfortably. The best advice concerning the backhand lob is to practice both one-handed and two-handed shots. Use whichever feels most comfortable in a given situation.

Drills involving lob practice are included in "Drop and Go" on page 82, "Lob and Switch" on page 102, "Station Doubles" on page 108, and "Deep Lob" on page 114.

Smash

The smash is another shot in tennis that is important when playing at the net.

You need two important things to hit an overhead smash successfully: the

physical skills and the confidence. If you don't practice this shot you will not

be prepared for it in a match.

From the ready position at the net, the first movement involves turning the shoulders sideways to the net, and at the same time positioning both arms for the swing (1 and 2). This quick preparation will allow you to snap quickly at the ball or reach slightly behind you if the ball is not very high over your head.

Next is the positioning phase. This is most often the hardest part of hitting the smash successfully. Although the ball is hit fairly high into the air, you still need enough time to establish good position for the swing. It is difficult to have a good perception of where the ball will come down until near the end of its flight. Try to imagine the ball coming down into a basket that is sitting on your front shoulder. Time the swing by planting the back foot and rotating the shoulders forward (3 and 4) as the ball is falling into the contact location. Reaching up to a comfortable contact point while keeping balanced and timing the swing correctly will be achieved only if you have positioned the body correctly. The only way to improve this part of the smash is to continue to practice the shot.

▲ MASTER STROKE ▲

Every time the ball goes up over your head you don't necessarily have to hit it as hard as you can. You should smash the ball only when it seems like it will be easy to do so. Sometimes you need to let the ball bounce before smashing it; sometimes you have to run back and let it bounce then return it with a lob yourself; and sometimes it isn't high enough above your head to attempt a smash with a full swinging motion, and more of a volley motion should be used. Try not to go beyond your limits of just keeping the ball in play.

At the contact point, (5) the arm is at full extension and the legs have pushed the body upward so that all energy is focused at the end of the racket head—much like the feeling of cracking a whip. It should feel as if you can't reach any higher and you are up on your toes at the contact point. It is the same throwing type of motion as the serve. The arm pronates outward as the swing is made in order to flatten out the face of the racket against the ball at contact. The shoulders turn in toward the net throughout the contact point. The wrist and forearm snap the racket face down on top of the ball as contact is made. Try to keep the elbow up in the air a little longer than normal to ensure that enough downward snap with the forearm has been made (6).

The follow-through is natural only if the swing path has been followed correctly (7).

Spend some time practicing the overhead smash by hitting the ball to the left side of the entire court, and then to the right side. By alternating your targets you will learn to position your shoulders according to where you intend to hit the ball.

Smash drills are included in "Wall Drills" on page 58, "Grand Slam" on page 110, "Lob and Switch" on page 102, "Station Doubles" on page 108, and "Deep Lob" on page 114.

Approach shot

An approach shot is a transitional shot that allows you to move in from the baseline area to the net, in order to get into position to hit a winning volley. This is a very important shot that will either set you up for an easy put-away volley or, if done poorly, create a good opportunity for your opponent to hit an easy passing shot.

Jimmy Conners had one of the best approach shots of all time. He would hit this shot so well that it would very often put his opponent in trouble enough to where he would get an easy ball to volley for a winner. Many times a well-hit approach shot turns into a winning shot itself.

This is another shot that requires specific knowledge on how to hit it, when to hit it, where to hit it, and how to practice it. In this chapter we will explain how to hit it,

and when to hit it. Drills involving practice routines are shown throughout various chapters, but specifically in a drill called "Pass Out" on page 112. Once again a reminder is to continue to set up practice routines for each of the shots described in Chapter 1.

When your opponent hits a ball that lands on your side of the court and you see that it will move you inside the baseline, you have to decide immediately whether you will

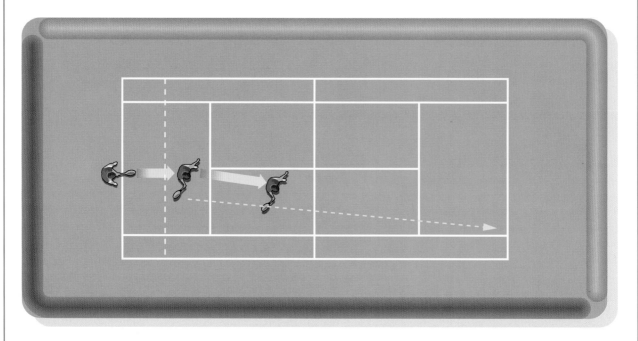

ABOVE **This diagram shows the imaginary line on the court where there is no turning back to the baseline. This "point of no return" or "no-man's land" is about halfway between the baseline and the service line.**

Running back to the baseline from beyond this imaginary line doesn't normally allow time to set up a good recovery position for the next shot.

hit your next shot and then step back behind the baseline, or hit an approach shot and proceed toward the net. There comes a point on the court where you don't really have a choice but to continue moving forward to the net.

At the highest level of tennis most players will try to get to the net as soon as the situation allows them to, especially in doubles. However, going to the net in singles isn't always a great idea if you are attempting to run in from near the baseline and you follow this up with a weak approach shot.

1 **2** **3**

When positioned at the baseline, you will want to be expecting a short ball at any time. Therefore, you must be on your toes and have your knees bent. As soon as the ball leaves your opponent's racket you should determine if the ball will land short and then immediately move forward toward the ball (1 and 2). As you close in on the ball you have to prepare the shoulders before it gets too late (3).

▼ FAULT FINDER ▼

One of the most common mistakes occurs when a player does not stop long enough to establish his balance before hitting the ball. This happens when a player continues to run while attempting the shot. Sometimes, however, if you are in a hurry you will not have a choice.

Another mistake occurs when a player has prepared for the shot by bringing the racket back too far, a habit that comes from hitting the majority of shots from the baseline. Too much of a backswing from inside the baseline will very often send the ball to the back fence.

▲ **MASTER STROKE** ▲

A good rule of thumb is to try to move up to a court position halfway between the service line and the net. Any closer to the net and the ball will go over your head rather easily—a smart opponent will certainly take advantage of this. Remember that you will always need to take a split step right before your opponent hits the ball. This means that, if you have not got to the ideal halfway point between the net and service line, you must take a split step regardless of your position on the court. A split step allows you to balance at the exact time that your opponent makes contact so that you will be able to move quickly toward the direction of the ball as it comes off the racket.

4   **5**   **6**

A good general rule to follow when shortening the backswing (4) is: The closer to the net you are and the lower the contact point you intend to have, the shorter the backswing should be. One common mistake occurs on this shot when a player completely stops during the swing. This results in no forward momentum during the swing and no continuation toward the net, so you slow down. You have to hurry upon completion of this shot so that you will not be too far from the net when your opponent returns the ball.

I like to refer to this brief slowing-down period to establish good balance as a "stop, step, and hit" (3, 4, and 5). The "stop, step, and hit" rule will allow for continuation to occur after contact is made so that you can get into a good volley position before your partner makes contact with the ball. Be sure, however, that you finish your swing before moving forward (6).

AGGRESSIVE APPROACH SHOT

One version of the approach shot that will help you hit the ball more aggressively without much more risk is to attempt to contact the ball at a higher point on the bounce than normal. This is usually around shoulder height (see right) and will allow you to hit down on the ball as contact is made. In this case, the backswing should not drop below the ball before contact is made.

The racket face should scrape across the top of the ball at contact. This forces the ball downward while imparting topspin to the ball. The key to this shot is not to let the ball drop down below the height of the net at contact. You will need to hurry to get close enough to the ball before it drops down too low. Use an eastern forehand grip or a western grip for this shot when the ball bounces high. A hammer grip will not work on this shot if you contact the ball from above the waist. It is very important that you choose the right grip for the height of the bounce.

BACKHAND APPROACH SHOT

Most approach shots are hit on the forehand side. If the ball comes down the center of the court directly in front of you, you should move into a forehand position to hit it. The forehand approach shot is a much stronger shot than the backhand, and is easier to position for as well. However, there will be situations where a backhand approach shot is necessary. Because of the physical characteristics of the body, the backhand requires a bigger shoulder turn than the forehand, and you will need to twist in the reverse direction in order to hit the ball with speed.

Most players therefore hit the backhand approach shot by "slicing" it. A slice approach shot will not require a very big shoulder turn, because of the backspin that is imparted to the ball. This backspin will cause the ball to float through the air and skip as it hits the ground. It is effective because it keeps the ball low and your opponent has to hit it upward on the return. This shot also lets you move through the shot as you swing, so you can move quickly into a good volley location. The demonstration for a backhand slice is shown in the backhand groundstroke section (see page 26).

This shot is emphasized in the drill called "Pass Out" on page 112 and "Crush" on page 80, and can also be practiced in the drills "Drop and Go" on page 82, "Short Stuff" on page 104, and "Station Doubles" on page 108.

Drop shot

An effective drop shot usually depends on how short it lands over the net, how much of an angle is used, how much of a surprise it is, and how fast your opponent is. Many times it is used in place of an approach shot.

A drop shot is a shot that you try to hit just barely over the net. It is usually attempted to try to win the point. Other times it is attempted to try and make your opponent tired, by forcing them to run in and hit it before the second bounce. Or it can be used to bring your opponent tó the net when you know they don't like playing there. Then you can use it with with a lob attempt over their head. This drives an opponent absolutely insane. But it is a good strategy if you don't mind making enemies. The best time to try the drop shot is when you want to surprise your opponent.

Trying a drop shot from behind the baseline is a high-risk attempt. The drop shot in general is not an easy shot: it is one that should be saved for a situation when you have a comfortable lead in the game, or in the set. A good drop shot is a ball that lands just over the net and is hit softly with a fair amount of backspin. However, I have seen recreational players hit drop shots that are often very effective without any backspin. Our discussion in this section will include the drop shot from the forehand side. A backhand drop shot is accomplished by applying the same principles as the forehand drop shot.

1

2

To achieve the surprise element of this shot, prepare for it as if you were going to hit a normal groundstroke or approach shot. Remember, however, that if you have moved inside the baseline you will need to shorten your backswing during

preparation. Choose either the eastern forehand grip or the hammer grip for the drop shot. Make sure the racket head begins the swing above the contact point (1). Just as you begin the swing, drop the racket face down by curling the

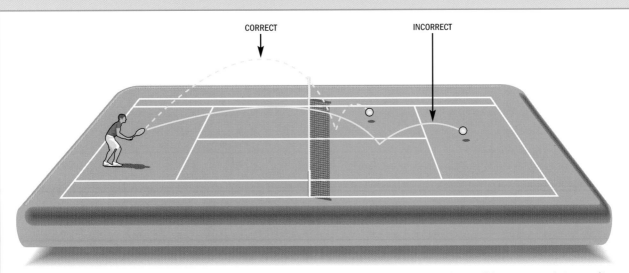

CORRECT   INCORRECT

ABOVE **A well-executed drop shot will travel only a foot or two above the net and have enough backspin that the ball will land inside the service line on the second or even the third bounce.**

The drop shot is not an easy skill to master. However, if you spend a little time practicing the feel of this shot you can gain confidence enough to use it during a match. It can become just one more weapon to add to your arsenal.

The drop shot can be practiced in the drill "Drop and Go" on page 82, "Opportunity Knocks" on page 94, and "Short Stuff" on page 104.

3

4

wrist and push the hand forward in a small arching motion. Contact should be made softly just around waist height (2). The racket face should scrape down the back of the ball to impart some backspin (3). However, just as the contact ends, the wrist finishes this scooping motion by lifting the ball from the bottom (4). This will make the ball lift up slightly so that it will come down shorter when it lands over the net.

Half-volley

A half-volley is not a volley at all. It is a shot that is hit immediately after the ball bounces. This shot usually occurs near the service-line area of the court. However, a half-volley may be attempted from the baseline on an occasional deep ball that you don't have time to back up on. In either case, it is a difficult shot to understand if you have never tried it, but with practice it can easily be mastered.

1

The first concept to understand is that there is essentially no backswing involved in a half-volley. Start by turning to the forehand side from the ready position, and dropping the racket head straight down directly behind the point where the ball will bounce (1). The ball picks up speed immediately after hitting the ground and therefore enough force is generated from the speed of the ball to allow it to simply ricochet off the strings as you carefully position the face of the racket (2). You need to contact the ball about two to four inches (5 to 10 cm) off the ground.

2

An eastern forehand grip will generally work best on this shot because it allows the wrist to reposition the racket face if at the last second you misjudge where the ball will bounce. A hammer grip can be used in some cases as well, especially if the contact point is further back. However, many times the ball tends to "pop up" using this grip, allowing your opponent at the net to hit an easy volley winner. If you are continuing to hit the ball up in the air, close the racket face more over the top of the ball on contact by using your wrist, or by changing your grip to the eastern forehand.

▲ MASTER STROKE ▲

If you are primarily a doubles player, you will need to develop this shot. Remember that your opponent is going to try to hit the ball to your feet as much as possible. When you are positioned on the court near the service line, or just inside the service line, it is usually better to step forward into the ball than to try to back up and hit it. Many recreational players make the mistake of backing up in this situation to try to play the ball as a normal bounce. Instead, hitting a half-volley will allow you to have good momentum into the ball as you contact it, and it allows you to keep your good forward position on the court as well. This is a defensive shot that you will usually want to return back to your opponent's baseline.

3

4

If the ball rises further than about six inches (15 cm) off the ground before contact is made it is very difficult to determine where the contact point should be. Letting the ball come up too far from the bounce is not considered a half-volley. This is known as "hitting the ball on the rise" and is the most difficult way to hit the ball after it has bounced.

The motion of the arm and racket during a half-volley is generally very short (3). It can sometimes be compared to hitting a ping-pong ball. The faster the ball is coming toward you, the shorter your "punch" forward will be (4).

If you are trying to half-volley a slower ball you will need to extend the follow-through a bit more forward to add some depth to your shot.

A half-volley on the backhand side will apply the exact same principles as the forehand side. However, an eastern backhand grip should be used.

This shot can be practiced during variations of the Chapter 3 drills called "Volley Rallies" and "Serve and Volley." A good variation is the drill in Chapter 4, "On the Rise." This drill will allow you to recognize and practice occasional half-volleys from the baseline area.

CHAPTER TWO

Target Drills

Although the game of tennis is being played at faster speeds now than ever before, the most important factor remains: you have to hit the ball where you want it to go. Many times I have seen two very different types of doubles teams playing a match against each other. One team will hit every ball as hard as they can, going for winners on almost every shot. The other team will simply hit the ball right where they want it to go. This will not be a long match. The best doubles players are the ones who are consistent at hitting the ball to an intended target.

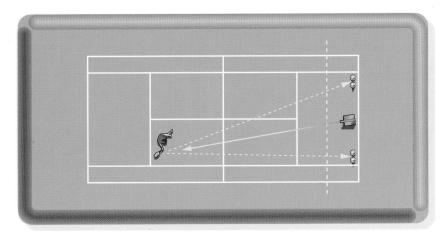

Deep - volley targets—*see page 64*

Hitting the ball consistently back into the middle of the court will win you a lot of matches. However, to advance your game to the next level, you will need consistency and accuracy as well. Proper placement can be developed only through practice and repetition. The drills in this chapter will provide you with some basic target practice to help improve your accuracy. You will need a few plastic cones, a long rope, or some type of target to aim for on the court. You will also need a good supply of balls and a practice partner to feed them to you, or use a ball machine if it is available.

Wall drills

Hitting a tennis ball against a wall can be a very effective way to practice some fundamentals of the game. It allows you to practice without a partner while you are able to focus on certain elements of your strokes that need improvement.

Many players feel that hitting against a wall is boring and has few benefits. Not so if you are able to vary your activity and you can understand the goal of the practice drills, you should benefit very well. The following set of drills will teach you how to vary your practice routines with the wall so that you remain mentally stimulated throughout. I don't recommend hours and hours of training against a wall, but including this in your practice schedule will help balance your overall game. The most obvious way to practice with the wall is to stand about 30 feet (9 meters) away and hit

With both variations it is important to keep in mind that you are trying to develop consistency and accuracy in your shots. You might ask how this can be done without a real court. Mark an area on the wall with some tape or a piece of chalk (1). By practicing hitting to this target on the wall you will be teaching yourself how to control the racket face with critical wrist adjustments at the point of contact. When this image of a wall target is transferred out onto the court, the accuracy of your shots will improve because you are now visualizing a target that is half the distance away from where the ball will actually land on the court. This philosophy is very similar to what professional golfers and bowlers do. An accurate short target will always line up with a longer one, and it is obviously easier to hit.

The next drill variation allows you to practice simple mechanics on the forehand or backhand volley. Position yourself about 10 feet (3 meters) away from the wall. Practice controlling your volleys by hitting them back to the same target on the wall (2). Remember to hit the ball softly enough so that you establish a rhythm to your practice. First, try to keep the ball on your forehand side while you strive for good stroke mechanics. Next, switch to the backhand side and repeat the drill. Finally, as your mechanics improve, step further back and mix up your shots so that you randomly hit forehand and backhand volleys.

groundstrokes. This is fine as long as you keep a few things in mind. First of all, by the time the ball comes back to where you are positioned it very often bounces too far or you don't have enough time to position yourself well enough to hit it after one bounce. The way to control this would be to hit the ball softly so that it bounces off the wall under control and you can hit it after one bounce. An alternative would be to move back another 10 feet (3 meters) and let the ball bounce twice. This simulates the amount of time that you normally would have on a real court during a baseline rally. It also lets you take a full swing at the ball. However, by allowing the ball to bounce twice, it lets you practice hitting only lower balls. Target your shots higher off the wall and add some topspin to the ball.

▲ MASTER STROKE ▲

Serves can be practiced very easily against the wall using the same target principle described in this section. Many times, a practice wall will already have the net line marked. Remember, if you hit a hard flat serve you need to aim the ball close to the top of this line or your serves will be going long when you move out onto the court.

3   4

"To practice shots that you have to move to, or hit on the run, stand diagonally right or left of the wall, hit to the center, and run to cover the angle you've created. Choose what would be down the line or cross-court targets and hit to them as called for."

Scott Murphy –
USPTA Coaching Professional

COACH'S *COMMENT*

Another shot that can be practiced against a wall is the overhead smash. Stand about 15 feet (4.5 meters) away from the wall and hit the ball down into the ground about 3 or 4 feet (about a meter) just in front of the wall (3). This makes the ball jump up in the air so that you can practice the fundamentals of the overhead smash (4). Be careful that you don't get too close to the wall, however, you may find yourself having to dodge your own ricochet.

Cross-court groundstroke targets

Consistency is important in tennis. When playing at the baseline you need to establish simple patterns with your groundstrokes. This means not trying to overhit the ball. These patterns allow you to stay safely in the point until a good opportunity arises. It is important that you learn to target your groundstrokes to the area of the court where your opponent will not be able to put you in a defensive situation. Hitting the majority of your shots diagonally cross-court will play it safe by keeping a wide-angled shot attempt away from your opponent. This is actually a neutral tactic, where you are staying in the rally long enough for your opponent to either make a mistake or give you an easier ball to attempt to put pressure on him or her.

Not all shots are quite the same. Some bounce high, some low, some have backspin, and some have topspin.

This drill is actually separated into three different patterns. The first one is set up for cross-court forehands. Notice that this player is left-handed (1). Position a few cones about 6 feet (2 meters) inside the baseline and about the same distance from the sideline. Place the ball machine in the center of the court at the baseline, or have your practice partner feed balls from this location. Simply count the number of shots in a row that you manage to hit in the area of the cones. As your consistency improves, make the drill more challenging by counting successive hits into a smaller target zone.

The second pattern would be to repeat the drill on the backhand side (2). Remember the goal of the drill is to keep as many balls inside the court as possible. Don't make the targets so difficult that they will take away from this goal.

You will have to determine which type of groundstroke you will use as soon as your opponent hits the ball. If you vary the amount of spin on your groundstrokes you will have more consistency from the baseline.

While practicing these simple target drills, try to have your feeding partner, or ball machine, deliver different types of bounces with various spins. Try returning the ball to the cross-court targets using various amounts and types of spin. Try to discover which ones work best on which types of bounces. Generally, a higher-bouncing ball is easier to return with topspin than a lower-bouncing ball. A slice backhand works well against a low-bouncing ball on your backhand side.

Remember that consistency is the goal in this drill. Attempt to get as many balls in the court as possible and as close to the target areas as well.

3

✪ VARIATION ✪

Place the cones closer along the sideline and more toward the service line to practice wider angles. Rope zones can be used as well.

The third pattern involves hitting cross-court from the backhand side, but using the forehand stroke instead (3). This drill allows you to practice hitting the forehand "inside out." This is a very effective singles strategy that keeps your opponent on the defensive by hitting the ball to their weaker backhand side while you use your stronger forehand groundstroke. The goal of this drill pattern is to hit the ball consistently to the target area, which would normally be the opponent's backhand. This is a common pattern with two right-handed players. The photo illustrates a left-handed player hitting inside out to the left side of the court. In a match situation, an opponent will eventually weaken enough to allow you to attempt a shot into the opening cross-court.

Down-the-line groundstroke targets

Attempting to hit the ball down the line in tennis is not considered a high-percentage, or easily achieved, shot. A cross-court groundstroke is a safer shot because the net is lower in the middle, the court is longer diagonally, and there is just more room in the court to miss your target area slightly. Down-the-line shots are extremely important, however, if you are attempting to hit the ball into an open court, or if you are trying to hit a passing shot. In singles, if your opponent hits an approach shot into the corner, the first place to look for an opening will be down the line.

In doubles, you will need to hit into the alleys occasionally in order to keep the opposing net player from poaching the middle of the court. Practice the following drills to improve your consistency on these difficult shot attempts down the line.

ABOVE If you have trouble hitting a backhand down the line, and many players do, a good opponent will know to attack your backhand and come in to the net.

"A down-the-line shot is essential to have in order to be an aggressive type of player. Setting up targets and practicing these shots with repetition is the only way to improve them. Remember, hitting down the line doesn't mean you have to hit the line. Give yourself some room for error."

Aleco Preovolos – USPTA Coaching Professional Mt. Tam Racket Club Larkspur, California

COACH'S **COMMENT**

✪ VARIATION ✪

If you are primarily a doubles player, place the cones in the alley and have the ball machine feed from a cross-court position while attempting to hit the shots down the line. Another effective doubles shot down the line to a deep target is an offensive lob over the net player's head. Remember, it is always a good idea to balance the practice routine to suit your playing style, skill limitations, and overall strengths and weaknesses.

1   **2**

DRILL

Place cones at different depths along the sideline. A ball machine or a practice partner should feed balls from the center of the court at the baseline. Attempt forehands down the line (1). Try to be as consistent as possible. Practice hitting the ball to various depths to help you control the shot for the situation. A passing shot in singles needs to simply "pass" the player at the net. It doesn't necessarily need to land on the baseline. However, if your opponent is at the baseline and there is an open court, or perhaps you are attempting to exploit a weaker backhand, you will want to practice hitting the down-the-line shot to a deeper target.

A more challenging version of this drill would be to attempt the down-the-line shot while on the run. Simply reposition yourself further from where the ball will be fed. Repeat the practice drill from the backhand side (2).

▼ FAULT FINDER ▼

The most common error when attempting to hit the backhand down the line, is contacting the ball too far out in front of the body. This is usually caused from not turning the shoulders back far enough and/or being too anxious to hit the ball. Try to get set to hit the ball as early as possible, and then wait until the very last second to contact the ball. Finish the swing with the head down and the shoulders rotating toward the target instead of off to the side.

Deep-volley targets

When you're playing from the service-line area of the court, many balls are landing down at your feet. This is very difficult to return effectively. Many players become too aggressive when they try to return this shot. The high-percentage play would be to control this shot by hitting it safely into the deep part of the opponent's court. This is an important shot because, first of all, this is exactly what your opponent is trying to do: hit the ball to your feet.

You need to know how to hit it (see page 34), and where to hit it. Second, if you hit a volley that lands too short, in either singles or doubles, your opponent will move in for a good chance at an easy passing shot. This mid-court low volley, which occurs frequently in doubles play, will improve only if you take the time to practice it. These simple drills and diagrams demonstrate where to hit this ball effectively and why.

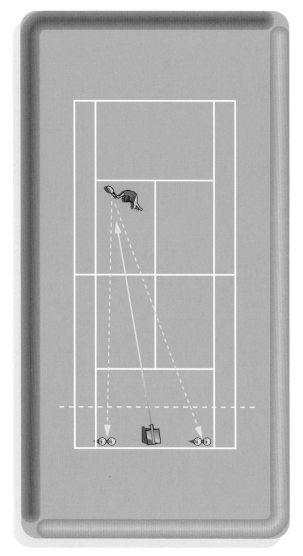

DOUBLES DRILL

If your partner inadvertently hits an easy ball to the opposing net player, you become a prime target. The reason the ball is hit toward your feet is so that, if you do manage to return it, it will usually "pop up" in the air, making it easy for your opponent to put the ball away (1).

LEFT **This is a drill from a doubles position just inside the service line. When playing doubles, you will be playing in this area of the court at the start of the point if your partner is receiving the serve.**

✪ VARIATION ✪

Mid-court low volleys are played very often in singles when a player is using a serve-and-volley strategy. Most top-level doubles players use this strategy as well. However, when you have reached a good position close to the net, it can become difficult to hit low volleys back toward the baseline. Another variation of this drill would be to simply move closer to the net and have your feeding partner, or the ball machine, feed low balls that just barely drop over the net.

Practice hitting the feeds away from the would-be player at the net by setting up cones in two corner positions at the baseline. A depth target can be made by placing a rope on the ground across the width of the court midway between the service line and the baseline (2). A ball machine or feeding partner should be set up near the baseline in various positions. Aim the feeds low enough to make the volley from below the height of the net. A situation such as this, where the ball is coming from the baseline, should allow you enough time to position the body well enough to ensure good fundamentals for a low volley.

SINGLES DRILL

This drill focuses on the singles position on the court. Practice hitting balls to the would-be backhand side of your opponent. The example shows a backhand target against a right-handed player. This is usually a weaker shot that will allow you to put away the next shot into the open court.

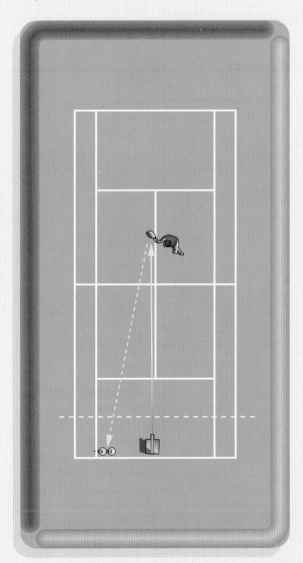

ABOVE **A deep corner target will force your singles opponent to move off the court and allow for an opening on your next volley.**

Angle volley targets

When you are at the net in a good volley position, which is about halfway between the service line and the net, you are anticipating an easy return from your opponent so that you can intercept it and volley it for a winner. Sounds easy? This is exactly what you are hoping for, an easy put-away volley. Easier said than done. This is where you really need to concentrate. Focus is usually lost to anxiety. When you get a ball such as this your job is to end the point – you don't want to give your opponent another chance. You need to practice hitting the ball where you want it to go, even when it seems easy.

When you are playing doubles at the net you will often face an opponent who is also at the net. If you get an easy ball about shoulder height, and your body is well balanced in the hitting position, try to hit the ball past the opponent closest to the net. This could be to the wide side of the court out of their reach (above), through the center of the court between the two players, or directly at the opponent's feet. If you hit your put-away volley back toward the baseline player, they will still have a good chance of returning it. By hitting the ball down to the feet of the opposing net player you will either force an error or cause them to pop the ball up in the air, which allows you another easy chance for a put-away shot.

"This drill is a classic example of a simple strategy that works almost every time. The idea of targeting the player at the net is very important. I have seen countless examples where my own students lose focus and volley back to the baseline player only to get burned with a subsequent lob."

Jorge Capestany – USPTA Master Professional
Grand Rapids, Michigan

COACH'S COMMENT

▲ MASTER STROKE ▲

The closer you are to the net when you volley, the more of an angle you have available as your target area. Experiment with these angles by moving your court position while practicing volleys within the service box.

DRILL

The diagram (right) illustrates the three targets on which to practice hitting the easy put-away volley. Have a ball machine or a feeding partner hit balls from the baseline directly in front of you. Practice hitting both forehand and backhand volleys to these targets from the right side (deuce) and left side (ad) side of the court. As you practice these variations you will notice that in some cases it is difficult to change the direction of the ball toward the target.

ABOVE **Angled targets let you practice hitting volley winners past the opposing net player in doubles.**

If you are a left-handed player and you are standing on the deuce side of the court (1), it will be difficult to hit a forehand volley toward the three targets to the left. You need to practice this shot by turning the shoulders all the way to the side during preparation and then contact the ball a bit later than usual. As you can see, it is also important to practice hitting target areas because your technique will change as well. Also notice that, if a ball is coming directly at your body while you are on the deuce side of the court, it would be better to move quickly to the left so that you could hit a backhand volley toward the left side (2). It is more natural for a left-handed player to hit a backhand volley to the left.

Remember that right-handers should reverse the application. On the ad side of the court the opposite is true. If you try to hit the ball to the targets at the right when the ball comes directly at you, and you are left-handed, it would be best to step to the right and hit a forehand volley. Right-handers will reverse this concept.

Serve targets

I had the privilege of hearing the tennis legend Stan Smith discuss the topic of the serve at a convention a few years back. He mentioned that the most important thing to develop on your serve is variety. This can mean different speeds, different spins, different serving positions from the baseline, and different targets. Now the spins and speeds may take some work trying to master, but the positions from the baseline and the targets should not. With a little target practice on the serve, you should be feeling more confident about getting the serves in at a crucial point in your match. If you practice hitting serves to only half of the service box, you can possibly eliminate an opponent's strong forehand return of serve by hitting it successfully to their backhand. Also, if you get used to hitting into half of the service box, you can imagine how big the service box becomes when you are just trying to get the ball in on the second serve. Using a good variety of serves is the key to keeping your opponent off balance and guessing as to which type of serve will be coming toward them. Let's face it, most of us can't hit the ball 100 miles per hour. If a player has only one type of serve, and it is a good one, it will be only a matter of time before an opponent makes an adjustment or two to figure out how to return it.

This serve drill is a common practice routine of every top professional player. There is nothing magical about any of the drills throughout this book. The pros are not doing top-secret drills somewhere on superior courts that nobody knows about. The only secret is that they have spent a great deal of time doing these drills.

▲ MASTER STROKE ▲

If you are having a hard time generating any zip on your serve you are not alone. One solution is to practice hitting the first serve as close to the service line as possible. This will make the ball bounce further back in the court, lessening the chances that your opponent will be able to crush the return of serve. Remember that you still have one more serve if you hit the first one long.

DRILL

Place three targets in the service box you are serving to. If cones are not available, stack four or five balls into small piles. Practice serving to the target areas from various positions at the baseline. Don't expect to be hitting the cones consistently. You are just trying to get the ball in the area of the targets. One variation of the drill would be to place a zone rope through the middle of the service box and attempt to hit each half of the box.

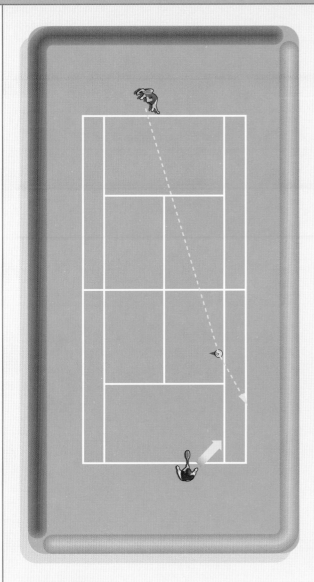

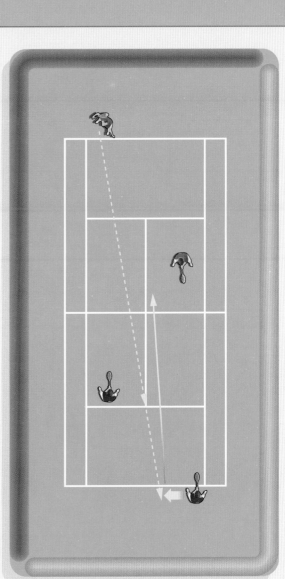

STRATEGY

Here we will discuss the reasons for serving to the three target areas of the service box. The first target we will discuss is the wide target toward the alley. This target is useful in both singles and doubles, but it is more effective in singles because it opens up the court. This leaves plenty of room to follow-up your next shot with either a groundstroke or volley winner (see above).

The diagram above illustrates the serve to the center T, where it can be used effectively against the opponent's backhand. This is effective in both singles and doubles, but it is most effective in doubles because it returns the ball to the center of the court. This takes away a good angle for your opponent to attempt a shot toward either alley. In turn it allows your partner at the net a better chance of getting to the ball because it will likely be returned to the center of the court.

ABOVE **A wide target shot is very useful in singles because it opens up the court.**

ABOVE **A center "T" target will keep the ball in the middle if the court and allow your partner at the net to expect a return toward the middle of the court too.**

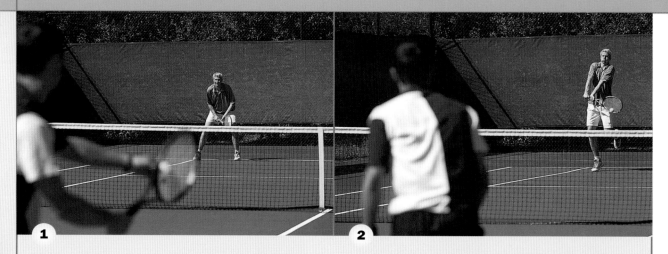

1

2

The third area of discussion is the target to the middle of the service box. This serve has the highest margin for error of course, but it can also be effective if the opponent has trouble establishing position on a ball that is hit right at them. Many

players who are very tall can reach a ball hit out wide in the service box, but they might have difficulty moving fast enough if the ball is coming right at their body. Serves to this area should be attempted with a good rate of speed (1 and 2).

A common mistake is when a player stands just inside the baseline and attempts to hit a volley when most likely the ball will land out of the court. So when practicing this serve drill, without a player returning the ball, it is easy to get into the bad habit of finishing the serve inside the court and not recovering back behind the baseline.

1

2

When practicing this drill, proper serve technique requires a bit of forward momentum throughout the serve motion. This usually carries your follow-through position inside the baseline (1).

If you do not intend to serve and volley, you should take a quick step back so that your ready position is just behind the baseline. This will allow you to reposition yourself well enough if your opponent returns the serve deep to your baseline (2).

ABOVE **The clash of the titans. Jim Courier versus Pete Sampras in the French Open 1994. This shows the sort of view that Courier had when returning Sampras'** hundred-mile-an-hour or more serves. Sampras' serving has proved a deadly accurate weapon on the international circuit.

CHAPTER THREE

Cooperation Drills

Consistency and accuracy can also be practiced with a hitting partner. Having you and your practice partner cooperate by hitting and returning in a predetermined way can establish a sense of rhythm in your movement to the ball. Also, as a result of this type of practice, you will develop the stamina that is required to stay in a point longer. This allows you to become more patient during actual match play and wait for the best opportunity to gain control of the point.

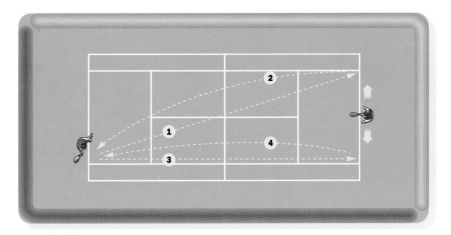

Groundstroke rallies— *see page* 76

The following section on volley rallies provides you with practice on quick-reaction volleys and half-volleys, which occur so often in doubles situations. These types of situations are often neglected during times of practice. It takes a proper balance of drills to develop a complete game. The drills described in this chapter will help to enhance your overall skills.

Groundstroke rallies

When you are playing a singles match, it is important to try to establish consistency in your shot routine. If you feel comfortable with your movements and your balance throughout the point, chances are good that your opponent will make a mistake before you do. With confidence at the baseline you will begin to feel like you are in a groove, that you have established a good rhythm to your movements, and you will feel as if you can get to any ball that your opponent hits. The following drills and their variations will allow you to work with a practice partner toward establishing this pattern of consistency.

DRILL 1

This drill pattern involves simply hitting the ball cross-court (above). This means from one corner of the court to the other, or diagonally. One player starts a rally by drop-hitting the ball from one corner of the court toward their partner, who should stand a bit toward the opposite corner. Assuming that both players are right-handed, each player will hit mostly forehands back and forth. There are a few good reasons to practice this cross-court pattern of play. First of all, it is a safer shot. This means that there is a higher-percentage chance that the ball will go in the court because the court is longer diagonally and the ball travels over the lowest part of the net. You will also begin to learn that by practicing angles on your groundstrokes, you can move your opponent around and possibly open the court up for a winning shot. Last but not least, hitting the ball cross-court from the baseline is what you would do in doubles almost every time. You and your partner can practice this doubles pattern by hitting cross-court groundstrokes while including the alleys. The idea of this drill is not to hit winners, but to keep the rally going while establishing good swing and footwork mechanics. The obvious variation of this drill is to reverse positions to the other corner and rally cross-court with backhand groundstrokes.

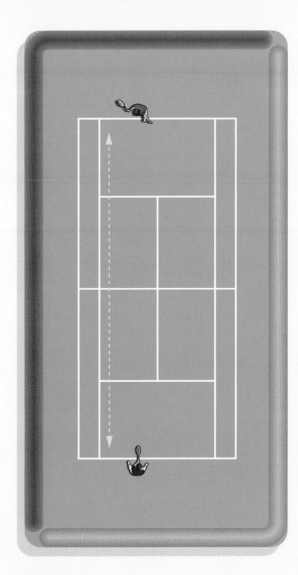

BELOW **Both players in this drill rally with forehand cross-court groundstrokes. Players should also practice with backhand groundstrokes as a variation.**

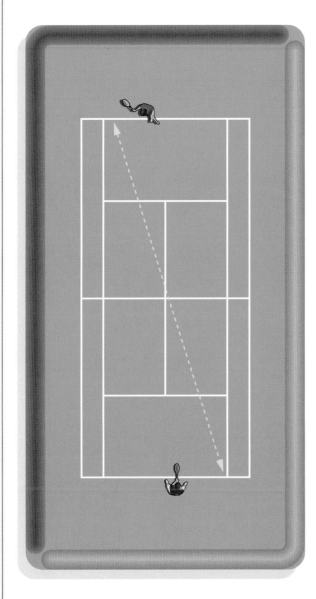

DRILL 2

This drill pattern positions both players on one side of the court while continuing to hit rallies down the line (see above). This is a lower-percentage, or more difficult, shot because of the higher net and shorter court length. This shot is not usually attempted unless you have decided to change the direction of the rally, or you are trying to hit into an opening in the court. But it is a critical shot when your opponent has moved up to the net and you are attempting to hit a passing shot down the line. So, you will need to have this shot in your toolbox. To increase the difficulty of this drill, try to hit each ball consecutively into the alley as you continue to rally with your partner.

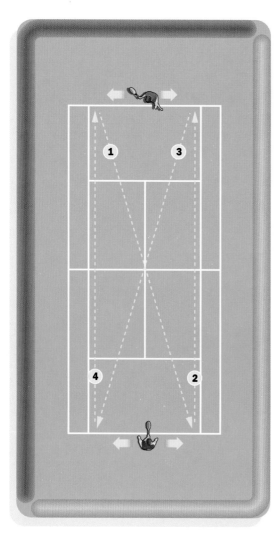

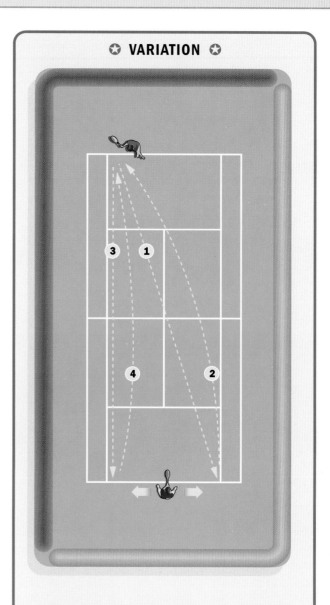

DRILL 3

This pattern combines the two previous drills by hitting cross-court and down the line in the same drill. One player attempts to hit every shot cross-court while the other player hits every ball down the line. This allows for continual movement at the baseline, establishing good footwork patterns while hitting on the run. You will probably be breathing a little heavily after this one.

FAR RIGHT **Russian star Yuegeny Kafelnikov with his powerful forehand groundstrokes made his mark in the French Open.**

A variation of the last pattern may help at least one player breathe a little more easily. One of the players hits every ball corner to corner, trying to move her partner across the baseline. The other player simply returns the ball to the same location every time. This establishes consistency of placement from all parts of the court. The player who is not moving should change her starting position at the baseline once in a while. When one of the players becomes tired you can reverse the roles.

Volley rallies

A lot of recreational tennis players I see practicing on adjacent courts spend most of their time hitting from the baseline. Although it is very important to practice groundstrokes, volleys are equally important, especially when you are playing more and more doubles. There are many different types of volleys: low volleys, high volleys, block volleys, drop volleys, and snap volleys, to name a few. The most difficult volley is the confusion volley. This is a ball that comes directly at you.

1

2

DRILL

Although you might feel like getting out of the way, there are certain ways to handle all these types of volleys. Some of them will feel a bit awkward even when you are hitting them correctly (1, 2, 3, and 4). You will need to practice volley rallies with a partner to be able to recognize these various types of shots quickly, and to get used to moving your body

correctly. The following drill patterns should help you gain more confidence when playing at the net. You and your partner should position yourselves about 4 or 5 feet (1.2–1.5 meters) inside the service line. Practice controlling the rally by hitting the ball easily enough that your partner won't have to move very much to make the shot. In other words, try to hit

✪ VARIATION ✪

A simple variation would be to have you and your partner move your court positions. Stand diagonally from one another in opposing service boxes. This reflects more of a doubles pattern at the net. Practice hitting to each other's feet, attempting to make your partner pop the ball up into the air so that you can make a more aggressive volley from a higher contact point.

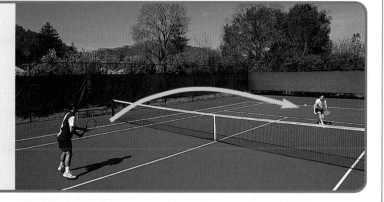

3

4

the ball to the same place every time. Remember that near shoulder level is the best height to contact the ball on the volley. By practicing hitting the ball to the same location every time, you are establishing good habits, consistency, and control. Before starting the drill, make a decision to hit your forehand volley to your partner's forehand, then vary the drill

by hitting backhand to backhand, and finally, alternating back and forth. Increase the difficulty as you improve your control. Eventually, you will improve your speed and awareness of how to handle these awkward volleys near the body.

NO-MAN'S LAND VARIATION

Although the zone between the baseline and the service line is called "no-man's land", it will inevitably occur that you have to hit the ball from there. Play in this position so that you get a feel for it. You will find that many balls will land right at your feet and will be hard to volley from that position. Many times you will need to hit a half-volley from this area of the court (see page 54). Position yourself and your partner in no-man's land and hit volleys back and forth to each other. Practice high volleys from this area of the court until you can hit the ball with control to the opponent's side of the court deep enough to continue moving forward to the net. This and the next variation are really the only ways to practice this shot and understand how it is supposed to work.

NO-MAN'S LAND TO BASELINE VARIATION

Now have your partner step back to the baseline while you remain in no-man's land. Try to hit every ball back to within 3 feet (1 meter) of the baseline. As a progression from this variation, you can practice moving forward after you have hit the first volley from no man's land, and then finish the rally from a position closer to the net. This repeats the situation for an approach volley, much like you would experience on a serve and volley strategy.

"Tennis training drills where players learn to volley back and forth to one another is the best way to master ball control. If you cannot hit the ball consistently right *to* someone, you cannot hit it *away* from them either.

Eric Johansson – USPTA Coaching Professional Cañon Swim and Tennis Club, Fairfax, California

COACH'S **COMMENT**

NET TO BASELINE VARIATION

The last variation positions one player at the net and the other at the baseline. This is also a very common situation in both singles and doubles. Good control and consistency are once again the goal of this drill. Try to have your partner at the baseline and hit all the balls to your forehand side for a while. Then switch to backhands. This establishes good fundamental habits. Now increase the difficulty by having your partner mix up the location of the shots. Eventually you can predetermine the pattern of shots to practice. For example, have your baseline partner hit a sequence of low volleys for you to practice returning deep into the court, then have your partner hit a higher ball so that you can attempt to

angle the volley away. A good progression from this drill variation is to start your position from the service line, hit the first low volley to your partner at the baseline, move in closer to the net, hit another volley to your partner, then have your partner hit an easy lob for you to try to put away with an overhead smash.

As you can see, there are many combinations and variations to create and practice. Being your own personal coach means that you have to determine the level of difficulty for the drill and the appropriate length of time necessary to maintain overall balance throughout your tennis development.

Crush

It is the perfect put-away situation. A ball that sits there close to the net after it has bounced softly on the ground. This is sometimes called a "sitter." You are almost drooling with anticipation. It is the easiest shot in the world. Then why do I see players blow this shot time and time again? It seems impossible to miss, but it happens. It goes straight down into the net, or you tap it back too lightly, or you slam the ball into the back fence. Once again, you have to practice this shot to improve your consistency. First of all let's make sure we all know exactly what type of ball we are talking about. This is usually a weak shot by your opponent that barely goes over the net, bounces pretty high, but not high enough for a full overhead smash type of swing.

Another common mistake would be to let the ball drop down too low after it has bounced. This doesn't allow you to hit the ball aggressively. You have to move up to the ball quickly enough so that you can hit it about head or shoulder height. This allows you to hit the ball hard and still maintain a good margin for error over the net. The following drill will help you practice this shot so that you will be able to "crush" the ball in no time at all.

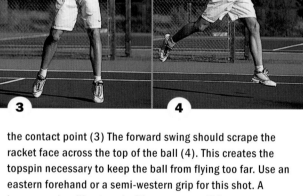

DRILL

Position yourself just behind the service line and slightly off to one side of the court. Your partner should stand at the baseline in the opposite corner of the court. Your partner starts the drill by hitting a soft and slightly high-looping ball just over the net. Move into position and crush the ball to the corner that your partner is playing. This way, your partner will be able to practice returning the ball as well. The ball should be returned the same way: soft, short, and fairly high. Many of the balls returned will have backspin on them. This will teach you how to deal with the spin after it has bounced. You must be completely balanced and correctly positioned in order to swing hard enough and still maintain control of the shot.

Adjust your swing so that the backswing doesn't drop below the ball. It should come forward at about the same height as the contact point (3) The forward swing should scrape the racket face across the top of the ball (4). This creates the topspin necessary to keep the ball from flying too far. Use an eastern forehand or a semi-western grip for this shot. A hammer grip will not work. Of course you will have to experiment with the swing motion and the contact point until you understand the concept well enough.

The concept of "scooting" forward just before the swing is a helpful tip to understand. Getting too close to the ball is a common error because many players misread the bounce and overrun the ball. If you have moved in from the baseline, try to slow down before getting too close to the ball so that you have control of your preparation(1 and 2), and then you will be able to scoot forward with the right amount of momentum and balance as you swing at the ball (3 and 4).

SKILLS PRACTICE

In most cases, you will have enough time to move your body into position to hit a forehand on this shot. It is difficult to accomplish this shot with a one-handed topspin backhand because it takes more time to prepare the shoulders, and it is also difficult to get the racket face over the ball at such a high contact point. A two-handed backhand, however, can be used more successfully following this concept.

As a variation, switch your court positions and aim for other locations on the court.

> ### ▲ MASTER STROKE ▲
> As the drill continues, it will be tempting to move forward and hit the ball out of the air as a volley. In many cases during a match, this is the right thing to do: volley the ball away for a winner. However, for effective use of this drill, let the ball bounce as often as possible. This allows you to work on the footwork elements that are so important to prepare your body position for the swing.

RIGHT American tennis star Serena Williams, who became the Wimbledon 2000 Women's Doubles Champion with her sister Venus. Her amazing power behind the ball helped her to take Olympic Gold in Sydney, Australia in 2000.

Drop and go

There is a specific strategy in tennis that will drive many players crazy. This is when a player hits the ball short so that you have to run up to the net to get it, and then they hit the next ball over your head and make you run back to the baseline to get it. After a few of these points you will be sucking wind like a vacuum cleaner. This is mainly a recreational level style of play. At the professional level it is used occasionally, but most pros are capable of moving in quickly to do something worthwhile with a short ball, especially if they know it is coming. Also, most pros are very skilled at returning any short lob with an overhead smash for a winner. Not all players are capable of hitting the ball short and deep all of the time. However, if you come up against a player who uses this strategy well, you will need to know how to keep up with them.

On the other hand, if you can master the art of the drop-shot-and-lob combo, you too can drive your opponent insane. This drill will help you work on this strategy, and against it as well.

COACH'S *COMMENT*

"The popular strategy of the drop-shot-and-lob combination can win points outright and effectively exhaust your opponent as well. In addition you have a good chance of winning the next point if you can quickly get your first serve in while you catch your opponent still out of breath."

Joe Dinoffer –
USPTA Master Professional
Dallas, Texas

1   **2**   **3**

DRILL

Both players start from the baseline. One player feeds the ball and the cooperative rally from the baseline begins. At any time during the rally, one predetermined player attempts a drop shot. This drop shot should be easy enough for the opposing player to reach. The return should then be hit back to the baseline player, who will then attempt a lob over the incoming player's head (1, 2, and 3). Once again, as a cooperative drill, this lob should be easy enough for the player to practice running back to the baseline to return the ball and then either play out the point or repeat the drop-shot-and-lob combination again. If this sequence of shots is repeated a few times during the point, you will be getting a good workout in the process. As you and your practice partner become more accustomed to this drill, you can alter the drill by implementing this strategy in more of a competitive nature.

1   **2**   **3**

SKILL

There are two things to remember when running back to retrieve the lob. First, always try to run well past the bounce of the ball, and slightly to the side of it. Many players don't realize how far back the ball will travel after it has bounced. By running slightly to the side of the ball you will allow yourself enough room to swing at the ball while rotating the body into a more comfortable hitting position (see diagram below).

Second, if you find that you are not getting back quickly enough when a deep lob is hit over your head, you should turn and run as fast as you can without looking at the ball until you feel you have run back far enough to get behind the ball, then you can look for the ball at the last instant before attempting the shot (see sequence, Photograph 2). This may seem difficult at first but should improve with repeated practice.

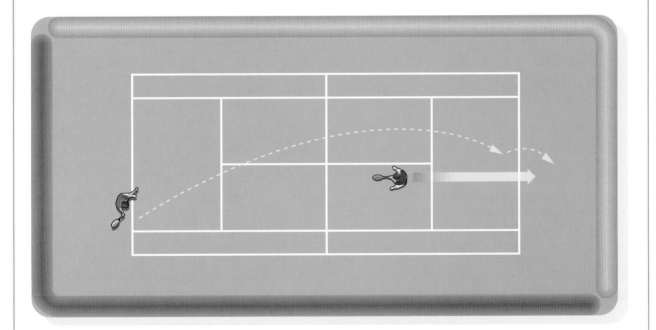

ABOVE **The thick yellow arrow shows the path you should take when chasing down a lob that has gone over your head and bounced deep in your court.**

Serve and volley

If you like to play at the net and you feel confident in your volleys, you will want to get to the net as often as possible. There are four ways to go to the net if you are at the baseline. The most obvious is when you get a short ball on your side of the court and you move in after hitting an approach shot. A second way to get to the net is when your opponent is in trouble. You have to be able to recognize this early and move in right away. A third, not so obvious, way is to sneak in when you see a ball being hit to your partner at the net. The fourth way to get to the net is to serve and move in right away. This is called serve and volley. This is not an easy strategy to master.

1

2

DRILL

Begin by practicing the serve-and-forward stepping pattern on your own with a basket of balls. Once you have become comfortable with this pattern, have your practice partner return the serve such that you can get to the ball easily enough to make the shot. Most of the time this shot will be an approach volley or a half-volley. Once you begin to have consistency in returning this shot, you can finish playing out the point with your singles, or doubles, practice partners. By having your practice partners cooperate with this drill, you will begin to feel the correct timing of the split step, how to move to the

The difficulty occurs with the shot immediately following the serve. A good opponent will know that they should try to hit the serve return back at your feet. This will be fairly easy to do because you have only enough time to move forward about two or three steps inside the baseline following your serve. If your serve is rather weak, it may not be a good strategy to attempt after all. However, with practice, and after becoming accustomed to hitting the ball from the mid-court area, you can improve your ability to get into a good volley position where you will have a better chance of getting an easy ball to put away.

3　　　　4　　　　5

ball once the return of serve is hit, and where to hit the ball to achieve the best results in singles and doubles.

This split step also prepares you to be ready to move in the direction of the ball as it is being returned. The split step normally takes place following the third step forward from the serve position (1,2,3,4, and 5). The timing of the split step is very important. If it occurs too early you will give up precious distance in front of you, thereby not allowing you to get close enough to the net to position yourself for an easier volley attempt. On the other hand, if the split step occurs too late, or not at all, you won't be able to move sideways to cover a passing shot, or backwards if your opponent attempts to hit the ball over your head. It will help your forward motion, and your chances of moving forward into the court, if you can toss the ball a bit out into the court for your serve. Immediately upon following through with the service motion you will continue to step forward toward the service line. Just before your opponent makes contact with the ball you will need to take a "split step" so your body becomes balanced (5).

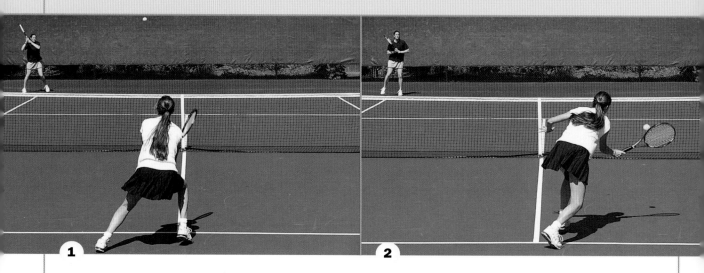

1

2

Once you have hit the ball from mid-court you will need to continue to move forward again and attempt to get into a

better volley position closer to the net. There you will once again take a split step as your opponent contacts the ball.

1

2

When playing doubles, you will most often want to hit this low volley back to the baseline player and avoid hitting it to the

opponent at the net. See the photo sequence for the serve and volley in a doubles situation (1, 2, 3, and 4).

▲ MASTER STROKE ▲

Remember that in order to be successful with this type of strategy you have to be sure that your opponent is not having an easy time returning your serve. So the first part of an effective serve-and-volley strategy is a pretty good serve. This is why you won't see a player serve and volley on the second serve as often as on the first.

3

4

This strategy is difficult because right after you serve and move in, you will be returning the majority of shots that have

dropped down to your feet. The ball is likely to pop up after you hit a low volley and a good opponent will know this.

3

4

⭐ VARIATION ⭐

In singles, you need to hit your mid-court volley well enough to put your opponent in trouble so that they won't have an easy time passing you on the next shot. You will need to practice this strategy a lot before using it effectively in a match. This drill will get you on your way.

CHAPTER FOUR

Strategy and Situation Drills

Strategy drills recreate certain situations in singles and doubles that are very common on almost every point. These drills need to be practiced in order to recognize the situations as they occur in a match. Many of the drills address the issue of a high-percentage shot versus a low-percentage shot. A high-percentage shot is an attempt that will be the most appropriate one in a given situation to keep the overall averages in your favor. A low-percentage shot includes any attempt at a very difficult shot. A low percentage means that most of the time the shot attempt is unsuccessful.

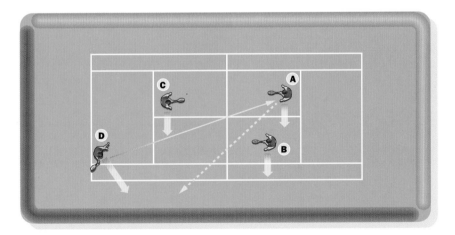

Alleys and angles doubles situations—*see page* 105

Many players will try a risky shot at the wrong time and in the wrong situation, or when they are hitting from an awkward court position. In a close match, playing smarter than your opponent will win you the match.

When the score is deuce, or you are one point behind at game point, play the point safely. If your opponent is going to win the game, let him or her beat you instead of beating yourself with a wild attempt at a winner.

"Open Court" singles strategy

Being able to move your opponent from corner to corner when playing a game of singles is a good strategy to try to wear them out. This can either lead to a weak return or open up the court for an easy winner. This strategy can be improved upon by practicing shots toward a shorter angle. The side T becomes a good target to use to move your opponent even more. The side T is the location of the court where the service line intersects the singles sideline. The diagram below illustrates the increased angle that becomes available by aiming for these short targets at either side of the court. This angle increases more when your hitting position is closer to the opposite sideline, and even more when you have moved slightly inside the baseline. Because this is a low-percentage shot, you have to wait for a good opportunity to hit it. The best position according to the diagram would be position C.

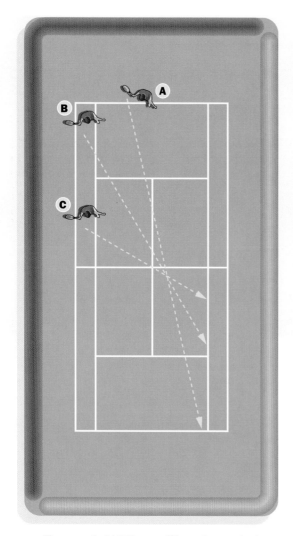

ABOVE **These varied hitting positions demonstrate the short angled results you can achieve against a singles opponent.**

1

DRILL

Start the drill with a baseline rally. One player bounce-hits the ball to their practice partner toward the opposite corner of the court. Continue to cooperate, hitting corner to corner until you or your partner feel you have a good opportunity to aim the shot toward the side T. This situation should occur when you have moved slightly to one side of the court, you are in a good, balanced hitting position, and you are able to move

You cannot hit the ball very hard unless a good amount of topspin is put on it. Also, it can't travel very high over the net or it will go out. The margin for error decreases when you're attempting to hit to this side target. The following drills should help you understand when to hit the ball to these targets while improving your consistency as well.

2

✪ VARIATION ✪

A more basic variation of this drill would be to have each player position themselves in opposing alleys just inside the baseline and attempt to rally cross-court to these short side targets. This makes it easier to establish a good hitting position. For additional awareness of the target area, use rope-zone targets to corner off the side T (see right). Practice partners can keep score of successful hits that land inside these zones. This can turn this into a doubles drill by including the alley as part of the rally and target area.

forward into the shot. It is never a good idea to try a lower-percentage shot when you are moving backward to hit the ball. You have to feel good about your position on the ball whenever you attempt a more difficult shot. The goal of this drill is to move your opponent out of the court so that you will have a chance to hit the next ball into a wide open court (1 and 2). However, many times a successful shot to the side T becomes a winner in itself.

"Opportunity Knocks" singles strategy

Following the serve and return of serve, most players in singles remain at the baseline and rally usually until someone makes a mistake. Eighty percent of points won in a tennis match are because of an error. So why not just keep tapping the ball back into the middle of the court? Well, against a good opponent, you won't stand a chance. A good player knows when and how to take advantage of a situation. This situation usually occurs when you move inside the baseline to hit the ball. Think of it as an opportunity knocking at your door. Hitting from inside the baseline gives you several options to choose from, hitting an approach shot and then moving in toward the net, attempting a drop shot, adding more speed to your shot, selecting a specific target to exploit a weakness that your opponent might have, going for a wide angle placement or short-angle target such as the previous drill, the open-court strategy (see page 92), describes.

BELOW **Various options become available when you move inside the baseline to take a shot.**

1 Drop shot
2 Add pace
3 Exploit weakness
4 Approach shot
5 Wide angle
6 Short angle

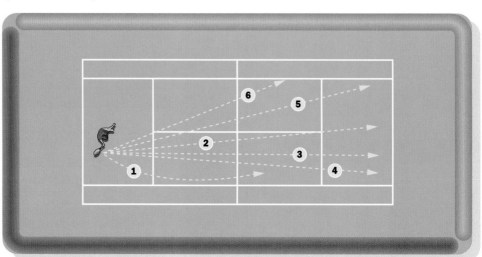

COACH'S *COMMENT*

"The next level of tennis is when you can force your opponent into making errors, and having a weapon where you can hit winners. This drill is realistic to actual match conditions. It teaches you to recognize the short ball and offers the option to go for a winner or advance to the net."

Angel Lopez –
USPTA Master Professional – 1995 National "Pro of the Year"
San Diego Tennis and Racket Club
San Diego, California

DRILL

Start the drill with both players at the baseline. Bounce-hit the ball to your practice partner and begin a baseline rally. Continue to rally cooperatively until one player hits it short enough that the other player has to move inside the baseline. This is the opportunity to attempt one of the options described in the diagram above. You need to decide as soon as possible what you want to do. Changing your mind at the last second is not usually a good idea. Practicing this drill will teach you when to go for it and when to stay in the rally. It will also help you determine from the options mentioned above which ones work well for you, and against which opponents. You will eventually become aware of which of these options you need to isolate and work on during your practice.

"On the rise" singles strategy

Hitting the ball as it is coming upward from the bounce is a very effective way to play in these times of fast-paced tennis. As a result, the ball is returned to the opponent's side of the court much sooner. André Agassi has developed most of his game around this style of play. The reason most people don't play this way is because it is probably the most difficult way to hit a ball bouncing off the ground. Right after the bounce the ball is traveling at high speed and it is difficult to time the swing because of the unpredictability of the bounce. The ideal way is to let the ball go through the full flight of the bounce and let it come down to a height near your waist before you hit it. This allows you to better position yourself as you have more time to focus on the ball and swing. Including this drill in your practice sessions, will develop your understanding of how best to use the "on the rise" style.

ABOVE **André Agassi hitting "on the rise."**

DRILL

This drill forces both players to hit on the rise by not allowing them to step outside of the court. Simply start a cooperative rally with a bounce hit. Both players position themselves inside the baseline during the entire rally. Play out points as you try to force your opponent to hit from deep in the backcourt. You are allowed to go to the net only if you move inside the service line to play the ball.

> ✪ **VARIATION** ✪
>
> Try this variation as an experiment: allow one player to move outside the baseline as he or she chooses, and see who has the advantage. At first it may seem as if the deep player will have the advantage until the player inside the baseline starts to learn how to hit on the rise.

"Inside Out" singles strategy

One of the most common strategies in singles that has developed at the professional level is the inside-out forehand to the opponent's backhand. This is a shot where the ball is coming down the center of the court, or slightly to the backhand side of a player who then moves their body completely around the ball so that they can hit it with their forehand. Most players, even at the pro level, feel that their forehand groundstroke is much better than their backhand groundstroke. Most of you reading this would probably agree. Therefore, by moving around the ball and avoiding the backhand, you are able to hit confidently with more speed and more accuracy. The intended target of the shot is usually to the backhand side of your opponent. By shifting your body around the ball and attempting to hit it cross-court in opposition to the way your body is moving, it usually forces you to change the path of your swing from inside, or against your body, toward the outside of your body. Hence, the name "Inside Out." This strategy is effective only when you are playing against someone who has the same dominant side as you.

Another situation arises from this when you move over to position yourself for an inside-out forehand and then your opponent attempts a backhand down the line. This is usually not a problem because many players struggle when trying to hit a backhand groundstroke down the line with speed and accuracy. This can still put you in a good situation, however, as long as you can get over to the ball quickly enough.

ABOVE **The German Women's Tennis heroine Steffi Graf hits a difficult ball "inside out".**

LEFT **Two right-handed players playing against each other. The goal here is to force your opponent to use their weaker backhand as you position yourself on your side of the court for a forehand. When this pattern begins, you will want to locate your recovery position a bit further over from the center of the court so that you will most likely receive the ball on your forehand side. Continue to hit forehands to the opposite corner into your opponent's backhand until you feel that there is enough of an opening on the opposite side of the court to attempt a winning shot.**

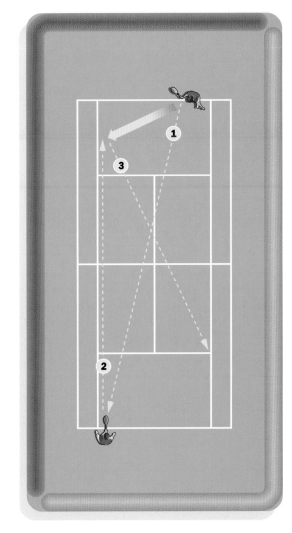

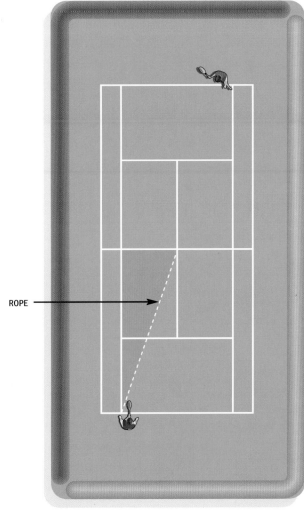

ROPE

ABOVE **By moving over to the same side of the court as your opponent, you now have a greater angle to work with in the open court, and you will still be hitting the ball with your forehand. It is always a good idea to make necessary adjustments in your game to counteract the way your opponent is playing. If your opponent hits a return down-the-line (2) you still have a chance to hit a forehand cross-court winner (3).**

ABOVE RIGHT **Section off the target zone on your opponent's side of the court with a rope.**

DRILL

Begin this drill with a cooperative rally from the baseline. Agree at the start of the drill that one player will be attempting to hit inside-out forehands to the other player's backhand. Continue to hit cooperatively in this pattern to become accustomed to the situation. After a few rallies, one of the two players can try to change the direction of the ball by hitting to the opposite side, and the point can be played out. Score can be kept to increase the pressure and roles can be reversed for each succeeding game. Use a rope zone as shown above to help you with your awareness of the target zone. This target area can be adjusted to fit your level of skill.

"Deep Trouble" singles strategy

When you are playing a singles match, it is very difficult to win points from the baseline unless you have incredibly powerful and accurate groundstrokes. Therefore, you must occasionally try to move up to the net and win the point from there. However, in singles, if you go to the net it is easier for your opponent to hit the ball past you, or over your head, if you're not careful about when you choose to go to the net. Of course the most likely time to go to the net is when your opponent hits the ball short on your side of the court. Another time is when your

opponent is in trouble. This could mean that they are on the run or that they are backing up when trying to make the return. Most often this return will be a weak ball that will land short on your side of the net. If you are able to determine immediately that your opponent is in trouble, you can sneak forward to a pretty good position on the court for either a put-away volley or a groundstroke winner. Many times this catches the opponent by surprise. They don't see you moving in because they are busy trying to get to the ball that you just hit deep into

BELOW **Playing forehand shots from the baseline are rarely point winners unless followed up with a move towards the net.**

their side of the court. By moving in, you can usually hit the ball into an open part of the court because they haven't yet recovered from the deep corner of the court.

The secret to this strategy is to recognize immediately that you have hit a ball that your opponent will have trouble returning and move forward right away. Whenever you hit a shot that you think will be close to the line, or you think it is possibly going long, instead of standing there watching and hoping, move toward the net. Your opponent is usually hoping the ball is going out too and won't play the shot as well as he or she should. The majority of times it will be a weak return. If you have moved forward you will be ready to play the short ball for a winning shot.

DRILL

In this drill, start the rally from the baseline with a bounce-hit. Both players should attempt to hit deep groundstrokes, with topspin if possible, within 2 or 3 feet (0.5–1 meter) of the baseline. Use a rope or chalk zone to mark off these areas just inside the baseline (see diagram right). In order to get used to seeing whether your shot will land close to the baseline, you and your partner should cooperate by calling "in" if the ball lands between the rope and baseline, "out" if it is just beyond the baseline, and "short" (or nothing at all) if the ball is in the court and doesn't make it deep enough to the zone. Try to guess where the ball will land as soon as you hit it. This will teach you to know when your shot is landing deep enough so that you can move in toward the net right away. Remember, your opponent's weaker side is usually the backhand.

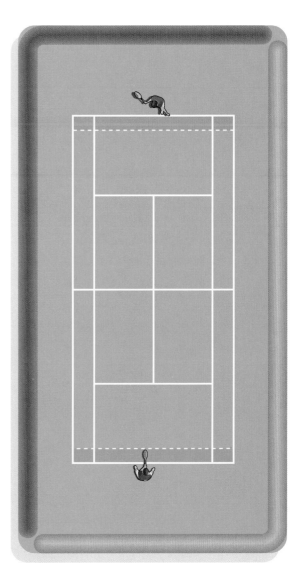

ABOVE **Use a rope to create a deep target zone. This will help you to identify times when you have a good chance to move toward the net.**

✪ VARIATION ✪

Keep score of this drill by allowing one point for each ball that lands in the zone during the rally, and one point if you win the rally. However, if your shot has landed in the deep zone and you moved in right away, you are awarded three points if you win the rally from there. Remember to try a drop shot once in a while or your opponent will get very comfortable hitting looping groundstrokes from a position deep behind the baseline.

Net-posts doubles situations

One of the biggest dilemmas I face as an instructor is trying to convince recreational players that moving toward the net is a good situation in tennis. This is especially true in doubles play.

Top-level doubles players will move into a volley area of the court almost immediately in the point. This is done following the serve and/or the return of serve. With both players at the net and in their correct positions, it is very difficult for the opponents to hit the ball between them or to the side of either player at the net. This is the dilemma, because now the recreational player will say, "Then they will just hit it over my head." Aha! That is precisely what an advanced player will be hoping for. An advanced player will have the skills necessary to end the point with

a well-hit overhead smash. Many players, however, will not attempt to lob at all. They will try to squeeze it in between the players at the net. This is why a well-developed volley is so important. When a volley is made in a comfortable position fairly close to the net and at a contact point above the height of the net, it can be hit almost anywhere into the opponent's court in an effort to end the point.

If the ball goes back to the baseline where your partner will be hitting it, you should drift back toward the service-line area so that you can protect the middle part of the court where your opponent might try to hit a volley on the return (see diagram below). This position is called the "hot seat" and is still a difficult position to play even when you are standing in the right place.

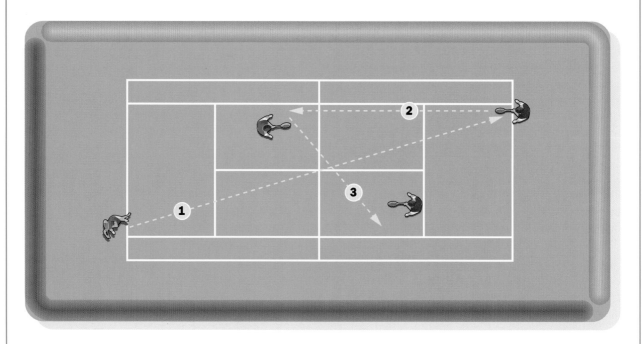

ABOVE **Proper positioning at the net is crucial when playing doubles.**

DRILL

Start this drill with a cooperative serve and return so that the two opposing net players get to practice moving forward and back at the right time. Remember that you need to move and then be ready when your partner is hitting the ball. Always take a split step right before your opponent makes contact with the ball. You don't have much time at all. One step forward or back may be all the time you have available, but this one step is still very important. It will also keep your feet active and teach you to be aggressive at the net. After a few rallies between the two baseline players, have one of the two players hit the ball toward the net player to determine if they have positioned themselves in the right place to make the best play on the ball.

When trying to position yourself at the net, a good rule to follow is to stand halfway between the net and the service line. Getting too close to the net will make it easy for the opponent to hit the ball over your head, and there is always a likelihood that you may somehow touch the net or reach over to make contact illegally on the other side of the net. There are always exceptions to these general rules, however: some players will never lob, or simply cannot lob effectively. If either case is true, moving even closer to the net may be a good position because it will be easier to hit a winning shot from there.

Playing halfway between the service line and the net isn't always the appropriate position, however. If your partner hits a weak shot to an opposing player who has moved up near the net, you most likely won't have a chance to defend against this ball if you are too close to the net. It will either get past you very quickly, or you won't have enough time to react if it is hit directly at you. The secret of playing successfully in the net position is to be in the right place at the right time.

The general rule in doubles at the net is to follow the ball like a magnet. If it goes to either side of the court, you need to move in that direction to either protect the alley or cut off any big opening in the court. It is also just as important to move forward and back when you are at the net. If you are standing near the service line when your partner hits the ball, wait there until it passes by the opposing net player. Then move forward quickly to gain a closer net position. This puts you in a better position to intercept a ball from the opposing baseline player. Remember to split-step before your opponent hits the ball.

Lob-and-switch doubles situations

One of the most common doubles situations occurs when the ball is lobbed over the net player's head and then lands near the baseline. Many times I hear recreational players say that it isn't a good idea to have both players at the net because of this situation. In some cases this actually may be true: for instance, when neither player is quick enough to run back to the baseline, or their overhead smash and volleys are not particularly strong.

However, top-level doubles players will get to the net as quickly as possible because it is the easiest position on the court to hit a winning shot. This winning shot is usually an angled volley or an overhead smash. If you are having difficulty with this situation, practice this drill to improve your skills in this area. This will stimulate better court awareness and establish the confidence necessary to advance your play to the next level.

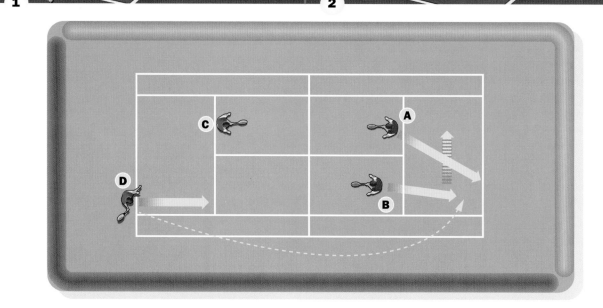

ABOVE **Players A and B switch sides if the lob lands deep. Players C and D move to the service line expecting a short return.**

RIGHT **Doubles team Swiss Martina Hingis and Russian partner Anna Kournikova playing a central ball.**

DRILL

This drill is started by having Player D feed a lob over Player B's head (see diagram). The correct strategy would be to have Player B move back and attempt to hit the overhead smash. At the same time, Player A runs behind Player B, not expecting that their partner will get to the ball. Player B should call "I got it" or "yours," as soon as possible. If Player B calls "yours" then the two players switch sides so that their court positions are changed. Players C and D should move to the service line on their side of the court and hope that the return is short. However, a returned lob is usually the reply (see photo sequence below). This is why they should position themselves at the service line. If it is a deep lob they can easily move back to get it, and if it is a short lob or groundstroke then they are close enough to the net to move in and put the ball away.

Short-stuff doubles situations

This is another common doubles situation with one player at the net and one at the baseline. It occurs when the ball lands just barely over the net somewhere between you and your partner. If you are at the net and the ball is hit short to your partner's side of the court, he or she may not be able to run up to the net quickly enough to reach the ball. Therefore, you will need to move to the other side and chase down the ball. However, many times you and your partner both run toward the ball and realize that either one of you will safely reach it (see below).

In order to avoid a collision, you must communicate with your partner. Usually the first player to call "I got it" should make the shot. However, many times both players are calling for the shot. What usually ends up happening is both players will stop at the last second and the ball is left untouched for a winner. The best approach is to continue to go after the ball once you have called it. However, in the situation that both players are calling for it, the player who is coming in from the baseline should take the shot. There are two important reasons for this. First of all, he or she will have the forward momentum to hit the ball. It is much easier trying to reach forward to hit the ball over the net than sideways. The second reason that the player coming in from the baseline should hit the ball is so that the net player can remain on their side of the court. Communication is the key.

DRILL

Start with a one-up/one-back formation on both sides of the net. One of the baseline players can begin the drill with a short ball between the two players right away. This will teach you and your partner how to communicate in various short-ball situations. After a few practice points it will be very easy for either player to get to the short ball because you already know that it is going to be hit there. It is always easier to get to a ball when you know what is coming. For the purpose of this drill, make sure that you position yourselves far enough from where the short ball will land so that you are practicing the communications and switches that are necessary. After a few points, as a progression from this drill, have the two baseline players rally cooperatively for a few shots until one player attempts a drop shot. This will create a more realistic situation that will surprise the opponents.

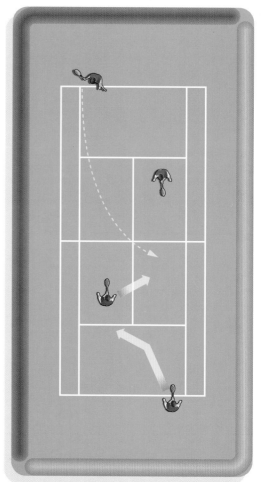

RIGHT **If the net player crosses to the other side of the court and attempts to make the shot, there will be a wide open court behind him. His partner must recognize this and move to cover this while calling "switch."**

Alleys-and-angles doubles situations

Whenever a player hits a ball on an angle toward the alley, it tends to open up the court for both teams. This creates an opportunity for the ball to be returned in one of three ways: down the line, up the middle between the two players, or cross-court on an angle toward the opposite alley. It is very difficult to hit a passing shot in doubles if both players are properly positioned at the net. This means that players should move quickly, in tandem with their partner, toward the side of the court that the ball is on. The first priority is to cover the alley because, if it is left wide open, this would be the most likely choice for the opponent to try a winning shot. If the opponent is crossing the singles sideline with their racket or feet, then you should take away the alley by moving well over to that side of the court (see below).

DRILL

Player D begins this drill by feeding a ball to Player A at the net, who hits a wide volley toward the alley. At this point, all players shift according to how wide the ball lands in the court. Player D looks for an obvious opening and attempts the shot. Practice this drill to improve your court positioning and reduce your opponents' chance to hit past you. This will open up the other side of the court for an easy winning volley.

COACH'S **COMMENT**

"The key to this situation is to try to make the baseline player hit the ball on the run. This will force an easy ball to put away."

Scott Borowiak –
USPTA Coaching Pro
Stockton, California

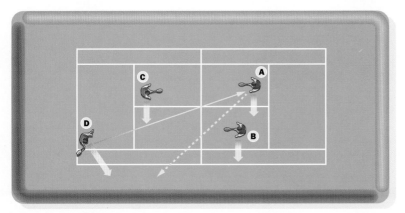

ABOVE **If the ball is hit in between the two players at the net it is the responsibility of the cross-court player, A, to cover this center of the court, and it will be the option for their partner, Player B, to intercept it and attempt a winning shot. The most difficult shot for Player D would be to try to hit the ball across to the other alley while on the run, and to hit it low enough for it to land in the short part of the court.**

CHAPTER FIVE

Pressure Drills

Practice is obviously very important to improving one's level of play in any sport. However, many players will practice without putting pressure on themselves. It is much easier to loosen up and hit with speed and go for corners of the court when you are just hitting back and forth without having anything to lose. It is amazing to see a player's game change when they begin to play a match.

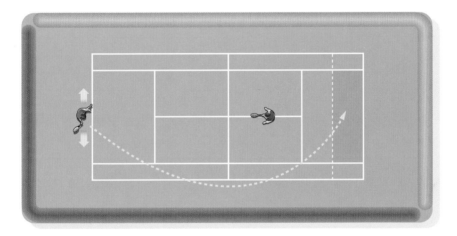

Deep lob—*see page* 114

You must set up practice situations where you can play under the pressure of winning and losing. If you are having trouble with a certain shot or situation, or you lack confidence in a particular part of your game, you can isolate this aspect in a practice situation. By practicing, and keeping score during the following drills, you will break down the points into specific areas of the game to work on while playing under pressure. One of the greatest opponents you will encounter when putting pressure into the game will be yourself. Being able to make good decisions and keep your emotions under control can make or break your entire level of play. The mental aspect of tennis is so important that many books have been written on this subject alone. Without opening up a giant can of worms here, it is important to point out that if you have a breakdown mentally, your actions will most likely fall apart as well. There is a fine line between understanding how to play aggressively while still being able to maintain control.

Station Doubles

This is a very popular drill for doubles players. It allows for maximum court movement, pressure, and intensity. This drill involves situations and shots from all areas of the court, which can make it a good warm-up exercise before a doubles match. One goal of the drill is to keep the game continuous. For this reason it is a good idea for all participating players to fill their pockets with as many balls as possible before the drill begins. Placing some additional balls up against each side of the net can help as well.

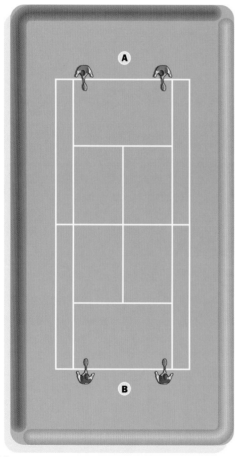

Station 1

Station 2

DRILL

There will be three areas of the court, or "stations," to begin each point. These three stations are baseline (1), service line (2), and net (3) (see above and next page). All players start the game from the baseline. One of the teams begins the point with a cooperative feed to either player on the other side and the point is played out. Once the ball is in play, players can move anywhere on the court. However, when the point is over, the teams must immediately move to the appropriate stations to begin the next point. Whichever team wins the point from the baseline (Team A) will move up to the service line and begin the next point with a cooperative feed. The point is again played out. If the opposing team wins this point (Team B) they move up to the service line and immediately feed to Team A, who must now move back one station to the baseline and begin the next point. If Team B wins this next point as well, they move up to

COACH'S **COMMENT**

"Without just playing a whole lot of points, there are very few ways to teach players to move properly and to make good shot selection in doubles. This drill presents the opportunity to do both and also teaches some of the needed skills for doubles that are otherwise only innate in some of the great doubles specialists."

Chuck Kriese
Men's Head Coach – Clemson University, Clemson, South Carolina

Station 3

After playing this game for a while, you will see that many of the court positions will call for certain obvious shots to be attempted. For example, if one team is at the net and the other team is at the baseline, it will usually be a lob attempt to start the point. This will make it more challenging to try to win the point from the net position. Another common situation occurs when both teams begin the point from the service line. It will be obvious that you must keep the ball low to the opponents' feet, and you need to be able to react quickly to the ball. These common situations make this a popular doubles practice drill with a good degree of pressure involved.

the last station on the court, which is the net position (center of the service box). Once again, they feed immediately to the players at the baseline and the point is played out. If Team B wins the point this time, they score one point in the game, and a new point is then started over with both teams returning to their original baseline positions. Remember to refill your pockets after each point is scored so that play can be as continuous as possible.

Grand slam

This drill involves two players starting a point with a specific shot, and then playing out the point. One of the most difficult shots to hit under pressure is the overhead smash. This is mainly due to a lack of confidence. Confidence comes from two areas: practice and determination. When you are playing at the net and your opponent hits you a fairly easy lob, you have to tell yourself immediately that you will take care of business and put the ball away. If you have doubt in your mind, you will either blow the shot or tap it back very softly. Practice will increase confidence because you will be more familiar with the situation. However, keeping score in this practice drill is important because it will also simulate real match pressure. This drill allows you to develop your overhead smash and increase your confidence as well.

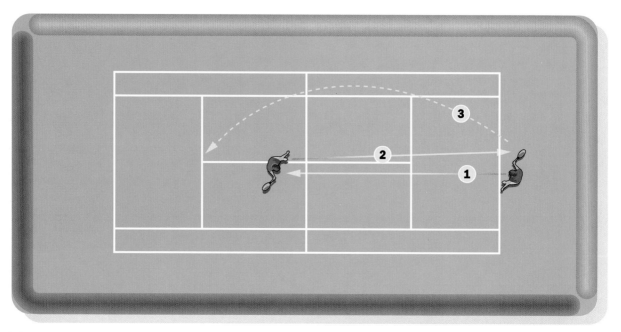

DRILL

Start the drill with one player at the net and one at the baseline. The baseline player feeds the ball to the net player, who hits a cooperative volley back to the baseline player. Now the baseline player hits a fairly short and easy lob for the net player to smash and begin the point. By making it easy for the net player to hit the overhead smash, it allows them to gain confidence. Pressure is added to the shot by keeping score. The first player to reach ten points by a margin of two wins the game. If the net player is doing what they are supposed to be, then they will win the game easily—this establishes the confidence. Players should switch roles after each game.

ABOVE **The point begins on the third shot of the drill – the lob.**

> ## ✪ VARIATION ✪
> You can vary this drill by making the initial lob a little deeper in the court. Try to determine how far back in the court that you can still smash the ball with good overall success. Many players have difficulty smashing the ball from beyond the service line.

▲ MASTER STROKE ▲

SUPRISE LOB VARIATION

Another variation involves additional cooperative volleys by the net player. A net/baseline rally is established until the baseline player decides to attempt the lob over the net player's head. This will make it more challenging for the net player because he or she will not know exactly when the lob is going to be coming. Keep score up to ten points and switch sides after each game.

The action photo illustrates this player using an advanced technique called a "scissors kick" to hit the smash. This allows a player to move back and jump backward slightly off of the dominant foot, then land quickly on the other foot. However, this advanced technique requires some athletic ability.

Pass out

One of the best situations to apply pressure during a point is when one player rushes the net after hitting an approach shot. In singles, it is usually best to try to hit the ball past the net player toward either sideline. The easiest attempt at a passing shot is usually down the line toward the side you are running to (see right). It is much more difficult to hit in the direction opposite that in which your body is moving. However, if you get to the ball early, you really have an advantage in that you can hit to either side

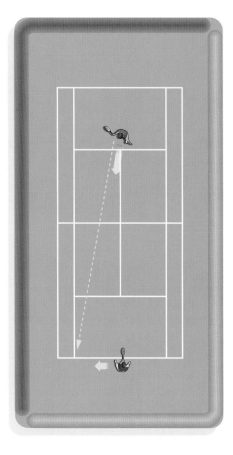

ABOVE **The main goal of the approach shot is to put the opponent in trouble. It is a good idea to practice this situation repeatedly, not only from the approach shot point of view, but also from the point of view of the player at the baseline. This player will need to remain under control during a desperate situation.**

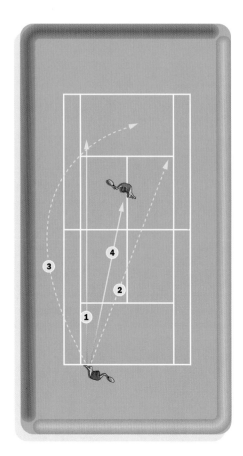

ABOVE **When you try to pass the player at the net cross-court you will have to angle the ball away from the player and hit it fairly low over the net (2). This is to ensure that the ball will not go wide of the sideline. See text above for a comprehensive explanation of all four options, as indicated on the diagram.**

of your opponent at the net. Your first option should be to look down the near sideline for an opening. If the net player has moved to cover this opening, you can try to hit the ball cross-court.

If you are the net player and you have hit the ball toward the sideline, you will need to move slightly toward that side of the court to protect against the down-the-line passing shot.

Your third option would be to attempt a lob over the net player's head. This can actually become a good first option if your opponent is crowding the net, or if they have a poor overhead smash. It is normally the safest shot to attempt if you are completely off balance, or you are desperately running to hit the ball. The fourth option is one that many times gets overlooked. Try to hit the ball just over the top of the net and softly enough to fall down at the net player's feet. Often this gives you another easier ball to hit because low volleys usually aren't hit hard enough or with enough of an angle to put the ball away (see diagram on opposite page).

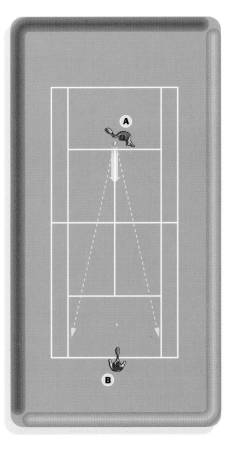

ABOVE **This drill can be started in two different ways. The first way would be to have the approaching player, Player A, feed the ball to one corner of the court on the baseline player's side, and then play out the point.**

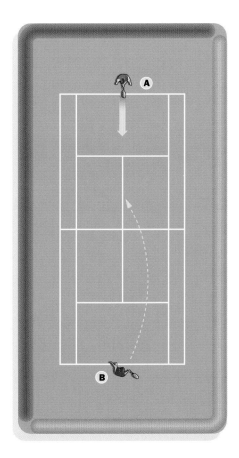

ABOVE **The other way would be to have the baseline player, Player B, feed the ball short to the other side of the court so that Player A moves in to hit the approach shot and then the point is played out. Keep score to a set amount and reverse roles after each subsequent game.**

Deep lob

Although it would seem that a lob is an easy shot to make, it is surprising to learn that many recreational players struggle with this shot. It is important to not only practice the proper stroke mechanics for the lob, but also to practice hitting them for depth, and while under pressure. If your lobs are too low or too short a good opponent will take advantage of the situation and put the ball away with an easy overhead smash.

BELOW **This drill creates a situation where you can practice various lobs while gaining confidence in your ability to consistently make the shot.**

DRILL

Start the drill with one player at the net feeding balls deep to either corner on the opposite side of the court. The player at the baseline should attempt a lob while moving slightly back and to the side. A rope zone should be placed on the net player's side of the court halfway between the service line and the baseline (see diagram). The goal of the drill is to hit lobs deep into the zone formed by the rope and the baseline. Pressure is added to the situation by allowing the net player to smash the ball if it is too short and then continuing to play out the point. Since the net player knows that the ball will be lobbed each time, he or she is not allowed to go behind the

ROPE

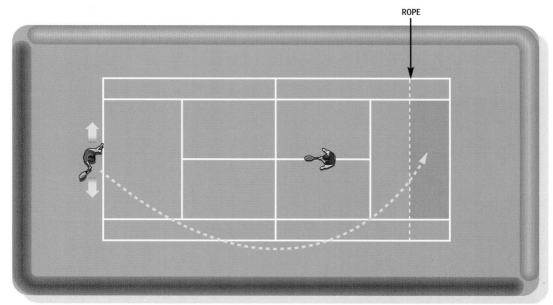

COACH'S *COMMENT*

"The lob is a key shot at club level for the simple reason that the majority of players struggle with the overhand smash. Many players tighten up when in a stressful situation such as having to lob over the net player's head. This drill will help you to get used to this situation and be more relaxed while hitting a lob."

Patrick Gillant –
FFT (French Tennis Federation)
Paris, France

service line to smash the ball. This increases the odds that the baseline player will be successful at hitting deep lobs. If the ball lands in the deep zone, one point is awarded to the lobbing player. If it lands between the service line and the rope, no point is awarded to either player. If it falls short of the service line, the net player attempts the smash without stepping beyond the service line. The point is then played out with the baseline player continuing to attempt a deep lob. Keep score to ten, having to win by a margin of two, and then switch positions for the next game. You can vary the level of difficulty by how the net player feeds the initial ball to the baseline.

Invisible Man

I introduced this situation to one of my students a few years ago during a private lesson. We were working on the technique of the serve. As my student became very consistent with the application of spin on the ball during the serve, it seemed as if she could not miss a single serve. She then told me that she always seemed to serve well in practice, but asked, "Why do I double-fault so much." Pressure? Maybe. Since this was a private lesson we didn't have an opponent to add to the pressure of the situation. As it turned out, we didn't need one. I simply told her to imagine an opponent ready to return her serve, and keep score of an imaginary game by hitting a first and second serve like you would normally do in a match, and alternate sides after each point. If either of the two serves went into the correct service box, she won the point. Easy, right? However, if she double-faulted once during the game she lost the entire game. She then played an imaginary set, which she lost 6–0. It was obvious that she didn't serve the same way as she did when she was practicing. She had nothing to lose and felt very relaxed while practicing. And yet, even without a real opponent, she still put all the pressure into her head that she was going to double-fault. Her worst opponent was herself.

Another realization occurred from this drill after she had gotten accustomed to the situation. She finally realized that no one was playing against her and that it was the sudden pressure of me telling her she would lose if she did not get the serve in. This led her to believe that pressure occurs with shock and that by spending time playing under pressure and becoming familiar with the situation you can overcome the fear of winning and losing. Try this one yourself and see if you have similar results.

LEFT **Mental fortitude and focus from American leading lady Venus Williams, the Wimbledon 2000 Women's Singles Champion and Olympic Gold Medal winner.**

CHAPTER SIX

Footwork

With the recent advancements in racket technology, more and more players are able to hit the ball with extreme amounts of pace and spin. While racket technology has helped speed up the game at the recreational level, touring pros have gotten bigger and stronger than ever before. In order to keep up with the increasingly high level of tennis that is now being played, top tennis athletes need to include a full strength-and-conditioning program in their busy playing schedules.

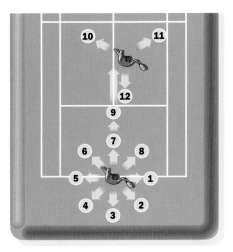

Split stop/ready hop—*see page* 126

Most pros on the tour today will hire conditioning coaches to assist them throughout the year so that they can incorporate these exercises into their daily routines. Once again, this is another broad aspect of tennis development that is so widely observed by players that entire books have been written on the subject and is way beyond the scope of this book. The intent of this book is simply to point out the significance of doing additional training drills in order to increase any player's level of skill.

The following drills focus on the development of proper footwork technique, and how to improve an overall level of quickness.

Basic training

Footwork is the name of the game in tennis. The key to hitting a tennis ball well is to be in a balanced position that allows you to take a full motion or swing, and to make contact with the ball exactly where you want to be in relation to your body position. There are a few basic patterns of moves that you can work on in order to improve your mobility toward balls that are a short distance away. At the baseline, the majority of balls hit to you are within approximately 10 feet (3 meters) of your starting position. Practicing these basic steps will improve your quickness to the ball while maintaining good balance throughout the point. An important thing to

Being in the ready position at the baseline means that you are ready physically and mentally. You have to be aware of exactly when your opponent is making contact with the ball. If you are on your heels when contact is being made, you are not in a ready position. A "ready hop" or "split step" is necessary to put you on your toes and prepare your legs for quick mobility.

If you watch professional players you can see them take this hop right before their opponent makes contact with the ball. This is especially evident on the return of serve.

This hop allows the legs to bend at the exact time that you will be making your decision to move in the direction of the ball.

This saves you precious time while trying to get to the ball early enough to maintain balance and establish forward momentum on the swing. By paying close attention to the sequence of photos, you will see that bending the knees allows you to move the inside foot first. This would be the right foot for a right-handed player moving to the forehand side(1). In this case, the left leg controls the distance that must be traveled to get to the ball by pushing off with that foot (2). This push from the outside foot generates from the knee bend, much like a spring mechanism, while establishing momentum in the direction of the ball. The next two photos show the left foot moving toward the right, (3 and 4) and then the final step where the right foot positions, or "plants," the point out in this exercise is that this footwork can be used only when balls are within a short distance of you at the baseline. Everyone will have a varying limit as to how far they are able to move by using this footwork. Any balls further than this 10–12-foot (3–3.5-meter) limit will require a cross-over step and sprint to the ball.

These basic footwork patterns can be practiced in your living room. The more they become your habit, the less you will need to think about your feet. Instead, you will find yourself getting into better position to hit the ball, and being able to concentrate more on your strategy.

foot into a good location to begin the swing (5 and 6). Altogether the right foot moves twice and the left foot moves only once. If you find yourself not getting close enough to the ball using this footwork, you have found your limit where you will be able to use this footwork pattern. However, if the ball is close enough to you and you can limit yourself to these few sliding or "skipping" steps, you will be able to get to almost any ball quickly enough and still have your feet in the right place to make a good balanced swing. If you practice getting into the hitting position before the ball arrives you will establish a good habit that will allow you an extra second to make any necessary adjustment steps. These last-second small steps may be needed if you have misjudged the ball due

to spin or wind conditions at that time. In any case, it is always a good idea to get to the ball early and have your racket ready to swing early as well.

Once you are in a good position to hit the ball, you can either step forward to hit the ball as shown in the photo sequence, (6 and 7) or simply turn from the torso and lean into the ball as you swing. This second option is referred to as an "open stance" and allows you to hit the ball without stepping in, thus saving a split second of time that you might not have against a hard-hitting opponent. Most top players today hit with an open stance because it saves time getting into a hitting position and allows for quicker recovery times.

BACKHAND GROUNDSTROKE

The above sequence shows the basic same footwork pattern to the backhand side (see pages 118-119).

STEP-AROUND SEQUENCE

The above photo sequence shows a player going through a step-around sequence. This right-handed player pushes back with the right foot while sliding the left foot over to establish a good hitting position. Depending on how much time you have available, some additional small adjustment steps may be necessary. The main goal of your feet is to

SHUFFLE-STEP RECOVERY

Moving back to the starting position is as important as moving to the ball. You need to recover quickly to get to the next ball. The footwork as described in this exercise is known as the shuffle-step recovery. Shuffle back to your original

move your body away from the ball, and then step, or turn into the ball as you swing and follow. Another variation of this footwork pattern is used very often when the ball is hit directly at your body. It may seem that this is an easy ball.

However, you will need to establish position quickly enough to allow forward momentum to occur during the swing. The change of momentum from the initial step back to the forward swing is difficult.

position just behind the baseline to face your opponent as you recover. This allows you to change direction quickly if your opponent hits the ball to the same side again. The same principles apply to both the forehand or backhand side.

Sampras drill

A few years back I had the pleasure of attending a one-day seminar which included not only the tennis legend Stan Smith, but also one of the top training coaches on the tour today, Pat Etcheberry. He spoke of his training sessions and programs with great pros such as Jim Courier and Pete Sampras.

It was interesting to note that he would always attempt to incorporate an element of fun in the workouts he would construct. It is always easier for everyone involved to work out when it becomes an enjoyable process, much as it is when playing the great game of tennis.

This is another excellent drill to help develop explosiveness to the ball. The most important step you will take toward the ball during a point, as far as quickness goes, is the very first one. This is provided that you have taken a "ready hop" and you are up on your toes as your opponent is contacting the ball.

1   **2**   **3**

One of the drills Pat talked about was a simple line touch drill used specifically by Pete Sampras. The drill begins with the player standing in the middle of the service box holding a tennis racket. A watch or timer is necessary to keep track of the total amount of time allowed for the drill, which is 30 seconds. The player moves laterally back and forth in the service box and touches the singles sideline and then the center service line. The player is not allowed to switch hands holding the racket or spin around in any way. This drill focuses on developing quickness during often-used side-to-side motions at the baseline by building muscles in the quadriceps area of the legs. Keep track of this drill by counting the total number of lines that the player can touch in 30 seconds. Then have the player rest for 30 seconds and repeat the drill. The 30-second time periods are used because of the similarity between playing out a point and the time allowed between points. You may want to adjust your time intervals, however. A recreational point usually lasts an average of 10 seconds. Endurance can improve with this drill as it is repeated on a routine basis.

Hot rope

For this drill you will need a rope of some type with a minimum length of about 6 feet (2 meters). Tie one end of the rope to either the net or the fence, approximately 4–6 inches (10–15 centimeters) above the ground. See if your score improves over the course of a few weeks. This will let you know that your quickness is improving and I'm sure it will be noticeable out on the court as well.

1   **2**   **3**

DRILL
Have a partner hold the other end of the rope so that it is the same height above the ground at each end. Your partner will also need a watch so that he or she can keep track of the 20 seconds allowed for the drill. As your partner says "go," you begin by jumping back and forth over the rope with your feet together. Try to jump as quickly as possible without losing control of your balance. Count the number of times you land on each side of the rope and total your score. Switch places with your partner and repeat the drill as often as you want.

RIGHT The American champion André Agassi covers the court with incredible speed and agility.

Obstacle course

This drill combines the development of quickness and explosiveness into one exercise that involves various footwork patterns. This drill allows you to establish good balance as you work on changing your footwork movements. You will need a few props to set up the obstacle course. A variation of this drill, if props are not available, concludes this section.

The props you will need are six to eight small cones, which can be purchased at most sporting goods stores, and six to eight small rubber or plastic pads. Small towels or old place mats can work almost as well, as would chalking up squares. Position the pads about 2 feet (60 cm) apart on opposite sides of the singles sideline (see right).

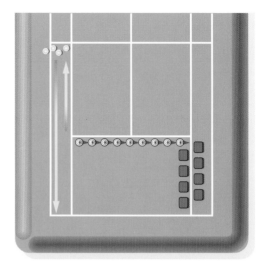

1

Start the drill in front of the rubber pads at the baseline. With your feet together, jump diagonally back and forth on each succeeding pad until you reach the end.

2

Next, you will jump forward and above each successive cone, also keeping your feet together as much as possible, until you reach the opposite alley.

All of the props can be adjusted to suit your level of ability. Place the cones in a straight line across the width of the court on the service line. Space these approximately 2–3 feet (60–90 cm) apart so that they are at a comfortable distance when you jump over each one. The last part of the obstacle course involves a sprint from the middle of the alley toward the net, where you will pick up a tennis ball from the ground and then finish the drill as you run back down the alley and across the baseline.

You will need a partner with a watch in order to keep track of the total time it takes for you to complete the drill. You can make this drill more challenging by adding a full second to your time for each obstacle you miss or touch inadvertently. Have your practice partner do the drill to add a little competition and repeat it as often as you like.

▲ MASTER STROKE ▲

If you do not have any props available you can simulate the movements by simply jumping diagonally back and forth over the sideline, and then jumping forward along the service line. Using tennis balls as cones is not advisable as it can become dangerous.

1

Next, sprint toward the net, crouch, pick up a tennis ball, and turn to run back.

2

Finish the drill by sprinting across the baseline, where your partner will check your total time.

Split step/ready hop

The split step and ready hop are so important in tennis that they should be emphasized in many practice situations. This footwork drill will remind you to split step at key times during the point. By concentrating on the drill without hitting balls, you will be able to focus on the proper footwork elements as you move toward the ball in various directions.

As your footwork habits improve, you can have a partner toss balls for you to hit as you go through the various directions toward each ball. It is a good idea to have worked on the basic training drill (see page 118) before attempting to do this one.

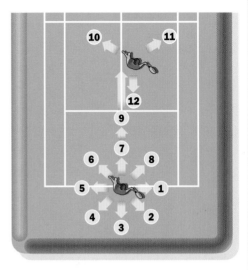

1

2

The drill starts out with the player holding her racket at the baseline (above). The first movement is the ready hop immediately followed by a quick lateral movement directly to the right (1).

Use the shuffle steps described in the basic training drill. Move through these footwork patterns as you finish each numbered direction with an imaginary swing. Upon completion of the swing return to the starting position using recovery shuffle steps and take a ready hop before moving toward the second location, which is slightly back, and to the right (2).

> ## ▲ MASTER STROKE ▲
> Proper footwork is not something that you have time to think about while you are playing a match. These footwork patterns need to become an automatic response for each situation. As these patterns become more familiar you can have your practice partner toss balls underhand, from the opposite side of the net, to each successive location to give you a more realistic view of the drill.

3 4 5 6

Progress through these first eight locations (3 to 6) and return to the starting position, emphasizing the ready hop each time you come back to it at the baseline. Remember that all of the motions in these first eight locations simulate balls that are within a 4–12-foot

(1.2– 3.6-m) radius of your body. These are the most common movements that you will make during the point. After completing Location 8 and returning to the starting position, simulate the footwork pattern used when moving up toward the service line.

9 10 11 12

This is a typical pattern when hitting an approach shot. As you approach Location 9, take the steps necessary when hitting an approach shot (9), complete the swing, and continue to move up to the next split-step location inside the service line.

Locations 10 and 11 will be imaginary volleys using the proper cross-over step involved to make the shot (10). Remember to take a ready hop upon returning to the start position at the net (11).

The final footwork motion involves moving backward as if the opponent had hit a lob over your head. Turn immediately, sidestep backward to the service line, and finish the drill with an imaginary overhead smash (12).

Practicing this drill on a regular basis will improve your footwork awareness as it moves you through the most common patterns during a typical point, and it will remind you how important it is to take a ready hop, or split step, after each individual shot.

Index